P9-DIB-902

Presented to the
Ironside Memorial Library
Bryan College
by
Dr. Judson Rudd

Race and Reason

A YANKEE VIEW

By Carleton Putnam

Public Affairs Press, Washington, D. C.

419 New Jersey Avenue, S.E., Washington 3, D. C.

Printed in the United States of America
Library of Congress Catalog Card No. 61-8447

FOREWORD

This book is a signal contribution to an understanding of the race controversy. No other writer, in my opinion, has yet combined so forceful an analysis of the viewpoints of both North and South with so clear a grasp of the reasons behind each.

Carleton Putnam strikes at the root of the matter. He thoroughly explores the ideology which led to the Supreme Court's decision in the desegregation cases and traces it to its source. In the process he puts race against the background of fundamental American ideals with arresting results. He presents documented facts, and discloses a situation, which I believe should be brought to the immediate attention of the American people. *Race and Reason* may well become a text for the unorganized majority in their battle against the social concepts of our minority groups.

If there be an argument in favor of integration which is not plainly set out in this volume, and as plainly examined, I have not heard it. The writing is incisive and can be read by the layman at one sitting with pleasure as well as profit. The author has thought through many issues, and has combined his thinking with careful research. He gives his results in telling sentences, crisp and spare. In these pages, any legislator, judge, lawyer, minister or college debater can have at his finger tips, conveniently indexed, a succinct reply to every sophistry advanced by the propagandist. To those who recognize that the salvation of the South lies in the education of public opinion rather than in rear-guard court actions, and that our national leaders must be told the scientific as well as the political facts of race, this book will be indispensable.

My personal enthusiasm has been increased by knowing Putnam himself. He is a dyed-in-the-wool Northerner, a New Englander collaterally descended from both Israel Putnam, George Washington's first major-general, and Rufus Putnam, founder of the Ohio Colony. Putnam is a Yankee in the true sense of the word. He speaks with detachment and from what I may term the native American outlook. Few men are better qualified by inheritance and training to recall us to the principles on which our republic rests.

In his own career Putnam has been singularly successful both as a practical man of affairs and as a scholar. Graduating with a science degree and with honors in history and politics from Princeton, and with a law degree from Columbia, he was for fifteen years president of Chicago and Southern Air Lines and later chairman of the board of Delta Air Lines. He finally retired, in his early fifties, to write biography, and has already distinguished himself in this field. My fellow journalist, Virginius Dabney, aptly described the situation when he said editorially that the first volume of Putnam's *Theodore Roosevelt* "had the critics turning handsprings".

Putnam writes from a knowledge of history, science and law. He writes from nation-wide experience in business, and from long residence in North and South. He knows America, its past and its present. I consider his message imperative reading for its own sake, and doubly valuable because of the man who speaks.

I would like finally to comment upon the panel of scientists who have signed the Introduction which follows this Foreword. Their tribute is, I believe, unique. I know of no other case where a social study of this kind has had such combined support from the fields of genetics, psychology, anthropology, zoology and anatomy.

The panel is headed by R. Ruggles Gates, generally acknowledged to be one of the world's leading human geneticists. Born a Canadian, Dr. Gates received his M.A. from Mt. Allison, his B.Sc. from McGill, his Ph.D. from Chicago and his D.Sc. from the University of London. He has been a Fellow of the Royal Society since 1931.

His active career began as a Lecturer in Biology at St. Thomas's Hospital in London, continued as Associate Professor of Zoology at the University of California, then as Professor of Botany at King's College, University of London, and as Honorary Research Fellow in Biology at Harvard. For the last eight years he has been engaged in world travel for the study of Races and Race Crossings. His publications include *The Mutation Factor in Human Evolution* (1915), *Human Genetics,* 2 Vols. (1946), *Human Ancestry* (1948), and *Pedigrees of Negro Families* (1949).

From the field of psychology we find Henry E. Garrett, Professor Emeritus, Columbia University. For fifteen years Dr. Garrett headed the Department of Psychology at Columbia. He has been President of the Eastern Psychological Association and the American Psychological Association. In addition he has served as Vice Chairman of the Division of Psychology and Anthropology of the National Research Council. He is general editor of the American Psychological Series, and is the author of *Statistics in Psychology and Education; Great Experiments in Psychology; Psychological Tests, Methods and Results; Psychology; General Psychology;* and *Testing*.

Robert Gayre is a Scot. Presently Editor of the *Mankind Quarterly*, he was formerly Professor of Anthropology and head of the post-graduate Department of Anthropo-Geography, University of Saugor, India. He is the author of *Teuton and Slav* (1944) and of *Ethnology*, 3 Vols. (soon to be published). He was Director of Education in the Allied Control Commission for Italy after World War II.

Wesley C. George began his career as Instructor in Zoology at the University of North Carolina, served variously as Professor of Biology at Guilford College, Adjunct Professor of Zoology at the University of Georgia, and Associate Professor of Histology and Embryology at the University of Tennessee Medical School. He has been Professor of Anatomy at the University of North Carolina since 1924 and was for ten years head of the department there. He is the author of numerous articles on the development of man and other vertebrates, comparative hematology and the philosophy of science.

There can be no doubt that the endorsement of these men, taken together with the evidence of other scientists called as witnesses by the author in his text, guarantee the scientific integrity of *Race and Reason* and confirm the soundness of its premises.

T. R. Waring

Editor, Charleston *News and Courier*

INTRODUCTION

Biological scientists seldom find themselves writing an introduction to what is essentially a study of a social problem. However, the problem in this instance is of such great importance from both the scientific and social standpoints, and the two are so closely interrelated, that we cannot dissociate ourselves from the task.

Our professional interest lies in the scientific foundations on which Mr. Putnam rests his thesis. We are in complete accord with what he has to say concerning these foundations. We agree with his balanced presentation of genetic and environmental factors in the area of both racial and individual biology. We believe they deserve this sharp reappraisal in the light of current problems in the world at large. We can also confirm Putnam's estimate of the extent to which non-scientific, ideological pressures have harassed scientists in the last thirty years, often resulting in the suppression or distortion of truth.

The intrusion of political thought into the social and anthropological sciences which has occurred on a massive scale during this period, has been a very great disservice to scientific investigation and to the guidance which scientific work and its conclusions ought to be able to render to human society. Man must be guided by science, but scientific thought must not be moulded to preconceived political ideas.

We, as signatories to this introduction, although we may differ over some aspects of genetic, biological, anthropological and sociological theory, believe that statesmen and judges today frequently take positions based upon an inadequate knowledge of the facts so far as they relate to the nature of man. Therefore, we have no hesitation in placing on record our disapproval of what has been all too commonly a trend since 1930. We do not believe that there is anything to be drawn from the sciences in which we work which supports the view that all races of men, all types of men, or all ethnic groups are equal and alike, or likely to become equal or alike, in anything approaching the foreseeable future. We believe on the contrary that there are vast areas of difference within mankind not only in physical appearance, but in such matters as adaptability to varying environments, and in deep psychological and emotional qualities, as well as in mental ability and capacity for development. We are of the opinion that in ignoring these depths of difference modern man and his political representatives are likely to find themselves in serious difficulties sooner or later.

Whatever may be said for or against minor or detailed points made by the author of this book, we feel that it deserves the serious attention of both scientists and public men wherever racial problems exist. The facts in it cannot much longer be ignored. It probes to the core of an abscess, yet does so with a healing touch. There is logic and common sense in these pages; there is also inescapable scientific validity.

R. Ruggles Gates,
M.A., Ph.D., D.Sc., LL.D., F.R.S.
Henry E. Garrett,
Ph.D., D.Sc.
R. Gayre of Gayre,
M.A., D.Phil., D.Pol.Sc., D.Sc.
Wesley C. George,
M.A., Ph.D.

CONTENTS

Chapter I

A FRAME OF MIND

When the Supreme Court reached its desegregation decision in 1954, not all of us stopped to think about its implications. There were many, of course, who were joyful. The Negro population and those white minority organizations which had played so large a part in pressing the case were elated. So were those good people who dream in general terms of pleasing everybody without counting the cost. But the majority of Americans, at least in the North, were preoccupied with other matters. They were surprised, perhaps a little startled, but quite willing to leave such a subject to the courts.

I confess that I was in the latter category. In those days, I was board chairman of a major airline, and such spare time as I had was occupied in beginning a four volume biography of Theodore Roosevelt. On the one hand, I was involved in a life of action; on the other, I was committed to the life of the mind, steeped in the moods of the nineteenth century, far removed from either action or the social trends of the mid-twentieth century. I cannot blame myself for not realizing immediately the meaning of the desegregation cases. Had I been resident in the South, it might have struck me sooner. But I was living in the national capital.

I speak of these things because the reaction, when it came, could not be unrelated to the personal equation. I believe that in 1954 I could lay claim to the viewpoint of an average American, a viewpoint in my case essentially Northern but modified by long experience in the South. In my early airline days I had spent seven years in Memphis, Tennessee, and had travelled extensively throughout all the Southern states, dealing with local governments, business groups and individuals in the most practical of activities. Twenty years before I had begun my airline career along the California coast by starting a service between Los Angeles and San Francisco. At a still earlier period I had gone to school for two years in Arizona, and I had spent many summer vacations in the northern Rockies.

In fact, to the American West I owed a large part of my life's motivation. From pack-trips across the Painted Desert in my college days, to camps in the Bad Lands of North Dakota where I began research on my biography of Roosevelt, I had known and loved the stage on which the pioneer played out the drama of the American Dream. It was not just a question of the sun setting beyond the Pass, nor the sound at night of wind rising in the forests of the Big Horn Mountains. These were important as symbols to the senses, but there were other scenes in the montage of memory—episodes involving people, from old prospectors and cowpunchers to women who had come to Arizona in covered wagons over the Santa Fe Trail—these were symbols of a different sort, figures of pride and self-reliance, and primordially American.

In a spiritual sense, of course, the Santa Fe Trail and the Oregon Trail had begun at Jamestown and Plymouth Rock, and had left me what I regarded as a personal heritage. My first American ancestors, on both my father's and my mother's side, had arrived in Massachusetts from England in the fourth decade of the seventeenth century. From Salem, to northern Vermont, to Saratoga and the Mohawk Valley, my father's people migrated to the West of their day and bequeathed me a proprietary interest in a sunset and a frame of mind. Call it individualism, say it was rugged, nonetheless it was American in its time. There were certain traditions that were taken for granted, yet which passed by osmosis from father to son. A man expected the community to do for him only what there was no way of his doing for himself. When he asked the community to do what he ought to have done for himself, this was begging; it was begging because it meant another's effort was making up his lack—and beggars were not popular on the frontier.

Nor was there a notion of equality in any sense except the equal chance. The frontier had its aristocracy of character to which one earned the right to belong. And the man with the bad reputation was not easily or quickly forgiven. I realize that today the frontier is history and that social conditions have changed. I do not see that the principles have changed.

Of my two grandfathers, one was a justice of the New York Supreme Court, another was a New York publisher who had the doubtful distinction of rejecting Mark Twain's first book. My father, who died young, was more adventurous. Having been cited for gallantry in action during the Philippine Insurrection, he remained in Manila to start the first American newspaper published in the Islands. There was something vitally American, in a turn-of-the-century sense, about my father—a certain gallantry, a gay initiative, a confidence in the strength of being right, and a willingness to take risks in its service. Once or twice he spoke with a twinkle of the close call I had had in getting into the world. Two years before I was born, he had come back to camp one evening from a skirmish at Tabuan and had found his undershirt cut across by a bullet.

Father was less fortunate in 1918. He died in the Argonne, and I went on to Princeton in 1920. I took a science degree, but majored in history and politics, because I wanted an education that would give me a perspective on the river of time, and I hoped a combination of science and history would provide it. So I began with astronomy, the story of the universe; went on to geology, the story of the earth; and finally to history, the story of man, elaborating the details through physics, chemistry and biology and flavoring the whole with some philosophy and considerable English literature. Perhaps it was a jack-of-all-trades education, but I cannot say I have regretted it. If I was vague about some of the trees, I believe I saw the outline of the woods.

Then came three arduous years which ended in a law degree at Columbia. From the law I acquired a wholesome regard for precedent. It is a lesson that can be learned from history, or from science, or, over a long life, from personal observation. But the law, I think, teaches it best. For a thousand years our Anglo-American common law has been based upon the evolution of man's experience in particular cases. Experience has produced the theory, rather than theory coloring the experience. In leafing through a book I wrote some twelve years later, I find the following record of my reaction to Columbia: "The American ardor for the new is one of the great hopes of the human race, but a respect for the experience of the past can, I think, contribute more to its fulfillment than the average American appreciates. For me, three years of saturation in the law did something to offset a very inadequate education in the classics, for it made real to me the substance of the soil out of which the present and the future grow."

Another fifteen years have passed since I wrote the preceding sentences, but I would now only re-emphasize, in an age obsessed with novelty and change, the importance of our Anglo-American heritage, particularly in the field of moral values and basic principle. There are very few social experiments that have not been tried before, and there are absolutely no principles that have not been thoroughly tested. "Winds of change" do not alter these.

If I were asked to be specific, I would say that as time has gone on, I have been impressed with two fallacies that have crept into the thinking of Americans: the fallacy that men by weight of numbers can defy the moral law and lean increasingly upon other men under the guise of the State, and the fallacy that this dependence is justified by the supposed right of all men to share equally in everthing. I shall have more to say on this subject later. My purpose here is to suggest the roots from which my views have grown.

It may seem strange, in the light of such views, that in June of 1954, when the Supreme Court's desegregation decision burst upon the country, I did not react at once. Surely, here was a sharp departure from the past—a confusion of equality of opportunity and equality before the law, with social and cultural equality—as well as a clear challenge to other American principles. My only answer, as I have said, must be that I was absorbed in other matters, an answer I believe I shared with many "average" Northerners. It took four years, in my case, before a chance incident brought the whole situation home.

I was thumbing through *Life* magazine for September 22, 1958, when I came upon an article by Virginius Dabney, editor of the Richmond *Times-Dispatch*. The article appeared to be a part of a debate which *Life* had arranged between Northern and Southern writers on the school integration controversy. It stated the Southern viewpoint most ably, I thought, but what really aroused me was something else in the same magazine. It was an editorial purporting to answer Dabney—an editorial wholly lacking in perception and full of inept analogies and abandoned principles. I was not by habit addicted to writing letters to the press, but in this case I could think of no better way to relieve my feelings. So I composed a letter of protest to *Life* and sent a copy to the newspaper editor I knew best. In my airline years I had shared some press flights with Frank

Ahlgren, manager of the Memphis *Commercial Appeal,* and he might be sympathetic. A few days later, *Life* answered with a polite acknowledgment, Ahlgren with an envelope enclosing a page of his latest edition. On it my letter appeared in full. It was a contrast that would grow sharper.

Then other things began to happen. Notes started to come in from old Memphis friends and from strangers. It was a comfort, they said, that at least one Northerner understood. Next, Dabney himself telephoned from Richmond. He had seen my letter in the *Commercial Appeal* and he asked if he might reprint it in his *Times-Dispatch.*

I hesitated for a moment because by that time I had had a chance to think further about the subject. There were several additional points I wanted to make. Moreover, there was one man who could do more to correct the situation than any other, if he would, and that man was the President of the United States. Perhaps, in the maelstrom of other problems and activities, he had overlooked the real significance of the desegregation cases. Perhaps, if others as well as I wrote him, he might be led to see the reasonableness behind the Southern position. Then from the pulpit of the Presidency he might enlighten the nation. I began to wonder whether the best contribution I could make might not be to try to reach him with a new letter, more complete than the one to *Life.* Meanwhile, as far as Dabney was concerned, it might be wiser for him to wait and see whether he preferred to publish the letter to the President.

Dabney agreed and I set to work, helped by an opinion of Justice Frankfurter in a case growing out of the Little Rock episode. Frankfurter's views, printed in the Washington *Post,* had spoiled my breakfast a morning or two before, but now they gave me a starting point. On October 13, 1958—I remember the occasion well because it was the climax of weeks of deliberation—I wrote as follows to President Eisenhower:

A few days ago I was reading over Justice Frankfurter's opinion in the recent Little Rock case. Three sentences in it tempt me to write you this letter. I am a Northerner, but I have spent a large part of my life as a business executive in the South. I have a law degree, but I am now engaged in historical writing. From this observation post I risk the presumption of a comment.

The sentences I wish to examine are these: "Local customs, however hardened by time, are not decreed in heaven. Habits and feelings they engender may be counteracted and moderated. Experience attests that such local habits and feelings will yield, gradually though this be, to law and education."

It is my personal conviction that the local customs in this case were "hardened by time" for a very good reason, and that while they may not, as Frankfurter says, have been decreed in heaven, they come closer to it than the current view of the Supreme Court. I was particularly puzzled by Frankfurter's remark that "the Constitution is not the formulation of the merely personal views of the members of this court." Five minutes before the court's desegregation decision, the Constitution meant one thing; five minutes later, it meant something else. Only one thing intervened, namely, an expression of the personal views of the members of the court.

It is not my purpose to dispute the point with which the greater part of Frankfurter's opinion is concerned. The law must be obeyed. But I think the original desegregation decision was wrong, that it ought to be reversed, and that meanwhile every legal means should be found, not to disobey it, but to avoid it. Failing this, the situation should be corrected by constitutional amendment.

I cannot agree that this is a matter involving "a few states" as Frankfurter suggests. The picture in reality is of a court, by one sudden edict, forcing upon the entire South a view, and a way of life, with which the great majority of the population are in complete disagreement. Although not from the legal, in fact from the practical, standpoint the North, which does not have the problem, is presuming to tell the South, which does have the problem, what to do.

To me there is a frightening arrogance in this performance. Neither the North, nor the court, has any holy mandate inherent in the trend of the times or the progress of liberalism to reform society in the South. In the matter of schools, rights to equal education are inseparably bound up with rights to freedom of association and, in the South at least, may require that both be considered simultaneously. (In using the word "association" here, I mean the right to associate with whom you please, and the right not to associate with whom you please.) Moreover, am I not correct in my recollection that it was the social stigma of segregation and its effect upon the Negro's "mind and heart" to which the court objected as much as to any other, and thus that the court, in forcing the black man's right to equal education was actually determined to violate the white man's right to freedom of association?

In any case the crux of this issue would seem obvious: social status has to be earned. Or, to put it another way, equality of association has to be mutually agreed to and mutually desired. It cannot be achieved by legal fiat. Personally, I feel only affection for the Negro. But there are facts that have to be faced. Any man with two eyes in his head can observe a Negro settlement in the Congo, can study the pure-blooded African in his native habitat as he exists when left on his own resources, can compare this settlement with London or Paris, and can draw his own conclusions regarding relative levels of character and intelligence—or that combination of character and intelligence which is civilization. Finally, he can inquire as to the number of pure-blooded blacks who have made contributions to great literature or engineering or medicine or philosophy or abstract science. (I do not include singing or athletics as these are not primarily matters of character and intelligence.) Nor is there any validity to the argument that the Negro "hasn't been given a chance." We were all in caves or trees originally. The progress which the pure-blooded black has made when left to himself, with a minimum of white help or hindrance, genetically or otherwise, can be measured today in the Congo.

Lord Bryce, a distinguished and impartial foreign observer, presented the situation accurately in his *American Commonwealth* when he wrote in 1880:

"History is a record of the progress towards civilization of races originally barbarous. But that progress has in all cases been slow and gradual . . . Utterly dissimilar is the case of the African Negro, caught up in and whirled along with the swift movement of the American democracy. In it we have a singular juxtaposition of the most primitive and the most recent, the most rudimentary and the most highly developed types of culture . . . A body of savages is violently carried across the ocean and set to work as slaves on the plantations of masters who are three or four thousand years in advance of them in mental capacity and moral force . . . Suddenly, even more suddenly than they were torn from Africa, they find themselves, not only freed, but made full citizens and active members of the most popular government the world has seen, treated as fit to bear an equal part in ruling, not only themselves, but also their recent masters."

One does not telescope three or four thousand years into the 70 years since Bryce wrote. One may change the terms of the problem by mixed breeding, but if ever there was a matter that ought to be left to local option it would seem to be the decision as to when the mixture has produced an acceptable amalgam in the schools. And I see no reason for penalizing a locality that does not choose to mix.

I would emphatically support improvement of education in Negro schools, if and where it is inferior. Equality of opportunity and equality before the law, when not strained to cover other situations, are acceptable ideals because they provide the chance to earn and to progress—and consequently should be enforced by legal fiat as far as is humanly possible. But equality of association, which desegregation in Southern schools involves, pre-supposes a status which in the South the average Negro has not earned. To force it upon the Southern white will, I think, meet with as much opposition as the prohibition amendment encountered in the wet states.

Throughout this controversy there has been frequent mention of the equality of man as a broad social objective. No proposition in recent years has been clouded by more loose thinking. Not many of us would care to enter a poetry contest with Keats, nor play chess with the national champion, nor set our character beside Albert Schweitzer's. When we see the doctrine of equality contradicted everywhere around us in fact, it remains a mystery why so many of us continue to give it lip service in theory, and why we tolerate the vicious notion that status in any field need not be earned.

Pin down the man who uses the word "equality," and at once the evasions and qualifications begin. As I recall, you, yourself, in a recent statement used some phrase to the effect that men were "equal in the sight of God." I would be interested to know where in the Bible you get your authority for this conception. There is doubtless authority in Scripture for the concept of *potential* equality in the sight of God—after earning that status, and with various further qualifications—but where is the authority for the sort of *ipso facto* equality suggested by your context? The whole idea contradicts the basic tenet of the Christian and Jewish religions that status is earned through righteousness and is not an automatic matter. What is true of religion and righteousness is just as true of achievement in other fields. And what is true among individuals is just as true of averages among races.

The confusion here is not unlike the confusion created by some left-wing writers between the doctrine of equality and the doctrine of Christian love. The command to love your neighbor is not a command either to consider your neighbor your equal, or yourself his equal; perhaps the purest example of great love without equality is the love between parent and child. In fact the equality doctrine as a whole, except when surrounded by a plethora of qualifications, is so untenable that it falls to pieces at the slightest thoughtful examination.

Frankfurter closes his opinion with a quotation from Abraham Lincoln, to whom the Negro owes more than to any other man. I, too, would like to quote from Lincoln. At Charleston, Illinois, in September 1858 in a debate with Douglas, Lincoln said:

"I am not, nor ever have been, in favor of bringing about in any way the social and political equality of the white and black races; I am not nor ever have been in favor of making voters or jurors of Negroes, nor qualifying them to hold office . . . I will say in addition to this that there is a physical difference between the white and black races which I believe will ever forbid the two races living together on terms of social and political equality. And in as much as they cannot so live, while they do remain together, there must be the position of superior and inferior, and I as much as any other man am in favor of having the superior position assigned to the white race."

The extent to which Lincoln would have modified these views today, or may have modified them before his death, is a moot question, but it is clear on its face that he would not have been in sympathy with the Supreme Court's position on desegregation. Many historians have felt that when Lincoln died the South lost the best friend it had. This also may be moot, but again it seems clear that for 94 years—from the horrors of Reconstruction through the Supreme Court's desegregation decision—the North has been trying to force the black man down the white Southerner's throat, and it is a miracle that relations between the races in the South have progressed as well as they have.

Perhaps the most discouraging spectacle is the spectacle of Northern newspapers dwelling with pleasure upon the predicament of the Southern parent who is forced to choose between desegregation and no school at all for his child. It does not seem to occur to these papers that this is the cruelest sort of blackmail; that the North is virtually putting a pistol at the head of the Southern parent in a gesture which every Northerner must contemplate with shame.

Indeed, there now seems little doubt that the court's recent decision has set back the cause of the Negro in the South by a generation. He may force his way into white schools, but he will not force his way into white hearts nor earn the respect he seeks. What evolution was slowly and wisely achieving, revolution has now arrested, and the trail of bitterness will lead far.

After dispatching this letter to the White House, I sent a copy to Dabney. Dabney allowed three days to pass out of courtesy to the President. Then he printed it on the editorial page of the Richmond *Times-Dispatch* and devoted his leading editorial to it. On the same page he included a cartoon showing the North being awakened from sleep by an alarm clock tagged "The Putnam Letter". Like the cartoon, the editorial was unduly complimentary. It referred to my effort as "one of the most incisive and convincing discussions we have seen". It dwelt on my training in history and law as well as my years of residence in the South and my New England origins. Finally it concluded: "The fact that Mr. Putnam has written this letter . . . is eloquent testimony to the fact that the South's case is getting across, at last, to intelligent Northerners. We still have a long way to go but we are making progress."

I took the personal references in this editorial with a grain of salt. I knew well enough that it was not Putnam but the predicament of the South that produced what appeal my letter may have had, together with the fact that I was a Northerner. But the response from Memphis, and now Dabney's remarks, made me wonder about something else. Here, in effect, was a call to the North for help, over the heads of the court, over the head of the President. Here was a great section of the country, more indigenously American than many of the areas most loudly denouncing the South, asking for understanding and aid. What sort of responsibility did this place upon me, and upon all impartial Northerners?

Day by day my concern increased. The effect of Dabney's publication was a new flood of letters, even of telegrams. If Memphis had produced a rain, Richmond produced a torrent. Dabney, too, was inundated. On November 4 he wrote me: "The response from individuals has been truly colossal. Nothing of the sort we have published in years has caused such a sensation." Neighboring newspapers started to copy, and mail began arriving from Norfolk and other Virginia towns. "The open letter to the President," said the Norfolk *Ledger-Star* on October 18, "has occasioned so much comment and brought so many requests for copies that the regular supply of back issues for that day has been exhausted. However, a supply of reprints of the page containing the letter is now available and copies may be had by writing or calling in person."

Referring to this announcement, a letter from Virginia Beach remarked, "During the ten years that I have been a resident of Tidewater Virginia this is the first time such an offering has ever appeared in either Norfolk newspaper. I thought nothing of a forty mile trip to and from Norfolk in order to purchase twelve copies. . . . Like yourself, I am a Northerner, a Chicagoan, educated at Williams College. . . ."

Actually, many of the letters were from native Northerners moved

South, and I hope I will not be accused of egotism if I say that most seemed to come from sane and earnest men and women. Few were from the group the Attorney General had said he thought was the source of all Southern opposition—"Crackpots running printing presses in cellars."

Several of my correspondents overwhelmed me with their courtesy and the courtly expression of their gratitude, although I knew that the praise was for a viewpoint, not for a man. As the letter began to be published more widely throughout the South, the cross-section of comments from all parts of the area had a common intensity. *Charlottesville*: "Permit me to say that, as a member of the School Board of this city, and therefore one more deeply and grievously concerned than even my fellow Southerners, your letter is the most thought-provoking and complete statement of the case that I have ever seen." *Birmingham*: "May I offer a toast to a scholar and an honorable gentleman and shatter the glass!" *Jacksonville*: "Your words so expressed my own views and opinion that I seemed to be reading my thoughts." *Columbia*: "I must tell you that that letter is the finest piece of logic and truth I've ever read; many I have talked with are thrilled with it." *Savannah*: "You have expressed so very well the feeling of Georgians, who love our country and also love our children." *Shreveport*: "The entire South is deeply grateful. . . . It is highly possible your efforts will be as fruitful for the North. You may be receiving the thanks of their thinking citizenship in the near future." *Meridian*: "Thank God for people like you. It does my heart good to know that someone other than a native Southerner understands."

These letters did not arrive by tens or hundreds; they arrived by thousands. College students wrote me they had framed the letter and hung it on the walls of their rooms. Schools assigned it for class discussion. Editors of law journals asked to print it. Judges wrote me from chambers. Senators and Congressmen simultaneously requested permission to insert it in the Congressional Record, and I was embarrassed as to the proper protocol in reply. The Birmingham *Post-Herald* alone supplied 22,000 demands for reprints. Whether or not I had the point of view of an average American on things in general, it looked as if many Southerners felt I had presented their viewpoint on integration.

Again I realized that my own efforts had had little to do with the matter. It was clear this time that the pent-up frustrations of the South had snatched at this straw because of its almost universal publication by the Southern press with favorable editorial comment. There were a few, but only a few, islands of silence where papers were in the control of so-called "moderates". For the most part, comment ran in the vein of Dabney's editorial.

Among columnists, the most active was John Temple Graves of Birmingham. Day after day he urged my letter upon his readers, upon the President, upon the North. In one of his syndicated articles he remarked: "What Carleton Putnam has written the President is newer than the New Deal, fairer than the Fair Deal, and as old as the Constitution of the United States. Let Southern young people be told. Let some of our Southern religious leaders be told, too."

Finally one morning my telephone rang and I found Graves on the wire from Birmingham. He wanted to know what reception my letter had received in Northern newspapers. I was compelled to answer that although Dabney had sent reprints to every editor in the United States only one Northern paper—a small one in Plattsburg—had printed it and with unfavorable comment. The sectional cleavage had been extraordinary.

Graves appeared shocked by this, and then an antidote occurred to him. He would call in his column for the starting of a fund to print the letter in the North by advertisement. He asked me if I would sanction such a move, and I replied that I had no objection, but that I could not personally be associated with it. He said he was in the same position, but that he would try to form a committee in Birmingham to receive the money and plan the campaign.

The upshot was the creation of what later became known as the Putnam Letter Committee, consisting of James E. Simpson, son of a former president *pro tem* of the Alabama Senate, Chairman; former Governor Frank Dixon; Lieutenant Governor Albert Boutwell and former Lieutenant Governor W. G. Hardwick. These distinguished public figures offered their services without compensation, not only to solicit and receive funds, but to perform the arduous task of handling what proved to be a voluminous and instructive correspondence—this time from the North. My own mail surpassed the flood from the South. The Committee's mail was many times mine.

The Southern press again lent their aid. An editorial in the Roanoke *World-News* was typical:

"We believe this plan to be a worthy one. Mr. Putnam's statement of the South's case deserves a nationwide audience. While it is true that he offers Virginia no quick way out of its present dilemma, it would be erroneous to say the letter is not constructive.

"In fact, we would say that the only hope of Virginia and the rest of the South lies not in 'massive resistance' but in persuasion, in logic and in salesmanship. The fact that Mr. Putnam wrote the letter is evidence that among some intelligent Northerners there is understanding and sympathy for the prevailing opinion in the South.

"More Americans need to know and understand this opinion for only by a change in national feeling can there be a real solution to the problem which faces us."

With the last paragraph in this editorial I heartily agreed. My observation of the manner in which "the paper curtain", as Southerners have come to call it, had fallen on my letter in the North and West was only a minor part of the pattern I was beginning to recognize. It was a small episode which provided a personal introduction to a wider panorama. I had said to the President: "From the practical standpoint the North, which does not have the problem, is presuming to tell the South, which does have the problem, what to do." I would soon discover that controlling forces in the North were not only telling the South what to do, they were refusing to let the Northern public even listen to the South's case. I would begin to harbor a suspicion, entirely apart from my letter, that in no other area of human affairs, at home or abroad, were so many people with no personal knowledge of a subject, and no practical concern in it, spending so much time dictating to other people, who had great experience with the subject and vital concern in it.

I would begin also, in due course, to understand the reason for this.

Meanwhile, the Birmingham Committee set to work. Within six weeks they had raised enough money, mostly from hundreds of small contributions, to place their first advertisement. It appeared in the New York *Times* on January 5, 1959, in a format six columns wide and a full page deep. To it was attached a coupon asking that readers who sympathized with the message and wished to see further advertising contribute to the fund. This procedure proved informative in itself. Each advertisement, as it appeared, brought in enough money *from the North* to pay for the next. Within five months the fund had passed $37,000 and the letter had been published in eighteen Northern and Western papers with a circulation of nearly seven million. Adding the initial free publication in the South, the total circulation had amounted to over ten million. I had no figures on foreign printings, but I was informed by the United States Information Agency that a paper in Salisbury, Rhodesia, carried the letter in full, and I had received comments from India and other remote areas.

Eight newspapers had refused to print the letter, even as an advertisement. These were: the Washington *Post*, the Los Angeles *Examiner*, the Los Angeles *Times*, the Pittsburgh *Press*, the Indianapolis *Star-News*, the Newark *News*, the Newark *Star-Ledger*, and the Buffalo *News*. None of the publishers of these papers felt able to give their reasons, but again, as my knowledge of the situation developed, they became clear.

The interesting thing to me was less the quality and extent of the paper curtain than the money the man and woman in the street were willing to pay to keep the advertisement going, and the nature of the correspondence it produced. Northern replies were ninety-five percent in sympathy. Public relations experts tell me that out of ten people who will write favorably on a subject only one will write when he finds himself in opposition, but even with this allowance, the man and woman in the street in the North seemed to be on the side of the South.

As to the unfriendly letters, they were the most significant of all. After a short time, I gave instructions to the Birmingham Committee to forward me no more favorable replies. All I wanted to see were the hostile five percent. Out of these I sought to distill some understanding of what was going on in the minds of the opposition behind the paper curtain. And the more I learned the more startled I became.

Chapter II

THE HIDDEN ISSUE

There were, of course, some violent letters from both Negroes and whites. There were a few from obvious crackpots. But by and large the disagreement seemed to be both sincere and emotional. It was impossible not to smile at letters from teachers and ministers who protested with incoherent emotion at the thought of my emotion, and who urged me to face the facts—which they had never faced themselves.

A scattering of superficial argument on a variety of subjects arrived daily: Did I not realize how unchristian my position was? Did not American democracy clearly require desegregation? Must we not set an example to other nations in the fight against Communism? Was not my position simply a revival of Hitlerism? These, and similar subjects, could be handled one by one without too long a letter in reply.

What I found of larger significance, because it seemed to be the common denominator in a universal misunderstanding, lay in what my correspondents called "modern" anthropology. Through almost all the letters that attempted really to reason, one consistent theme could be found: How could I be so dated in my thinking! Why was I still living in the nineteenth century! What was the point in quoting Lincoln and Bryce when everyone now-a-days knew they were obsolete! I could not help but remember a remark John Temple Graves had made to me concerning a debate on segregation he had had a few years before on the Town Hall of the Air. In it the opposition had continually harassed him with the comment, "Oh, Mr. Graves, if only you knew modern anthropology!" Mr. Graves, not being a professional scientist, had not attempted to meet this challenge in a Town Hall debate. But I was quite prepared to meet it in my correspondence. My only surprise was that it should need to be taken seriously.

And here I discovered an actual advantage in having separated myself for twenty years from the academic world and then returned to feel the fresh impact of what had happened in the interval. The process had its handicap only in a momentary disorientation. It had its value in a detachment of judgment and above all in a freedom from exposure to the creeping distortion of view, the slow but pervasive hypnosis, that two decades of ideological pressure can force even upon the sciences.

I had realized that there had been a broad movement to change man's concept of the nature of man. I had known that there had been pressure to widen the American doctrine of equality of opportunity into a doctrine of social, cultural, economic and genetic equality. By 1954 I had witnessed its invasion of the minds of Supreme Court justices. But I had not even then quite grasped how cleverly it had proceeded—infiltrating first the sciences that surround anthropology, moving next into the more strictly social sciences, enthroning itself at last in the Supreme Court's desegregation order.

Perhaps the whole progression should have been obvious to all of us, both within and without the academic world. What could have been more natural than that a movement calling itself, here, Communism, there, Marxism, somewhere else Socialism (but always having a base which I found easiest to describe by the word equalitarianism) should in its strategy include the subversion of sciences as well as governments? The same appeal to pity, to Christian love, could be used to make the fallacy more palatable. The underdog, who had been presented as invariably the victim of oppression, never of his own conduct, could now be made to appear the equal of all in innate capacity. It was the final, inevitable move in a deceptively false ideology—a move which in my opinion would prove the undoing of the whole crusade. A moderate amount of deception for charity's sake could be tolerated by all men of good will. No man of good will, once he was awakened to the truth, could tolerate Little Rock.

How this situation had slowly developed across the years was a long story. The immediate problem lay in the fact that my readers seemed unable to realize there was no such thing as equality even between two leaves on the same bush—that this was not just a matter of *difference,* but of *inferiority* and *superiority* in terms of the value judgments of persons, communities, nations, and cultures, and that the heart of the matter as regards race lay in the area of heredity. It had been essential to the equalitarian to denounce heredity in the biological phase of his subversion, and to make it appear that environment alone made the man. He had had to insist that nothing was innate, no capacity limited, all abilities unlimited, here and now, in this generation. If he could show that environment was responsible for all human differences, then a substantial part, although not all, of a brief for desegregation could be written. It was a strange program based on total error. Yet of all the chapters in the book of man's self-delusion none seemed to compare in its effectiveness with the current trance.

My task, therefore, consisted in trying to explain to my growing list of correspondents how seriously they had been misled, and the challenge was more complex than the queries regarding Christianity or Hitler. A long letter would be required in each instance, and there were hundreds to write. It was at this stage that I conceived the idea of addressing another government official, this time the Attorney General, and of distributing copies of the second letter to those who questioned the first—unless the Attorney General satisfied me that I had overlooked some important point.

The reasons for choosing the Attorney General were obvious. There was no individual in the government more charged with the responsibility of exploring the issues than he, appearing as he did as a friend of the court on behalf of the people of the United States. Perhaps he could explain to me what had happened, perhaps he had done everything in his power and had been over-ruled, or perhaps he could in some other way account for the extraordinary school decision. While the President was the man who could best break the public spell on this issue, the President could only do so if he realized the truth himself, and I was beginning to doubt that he did. The Attorney General, on the other hand, was paid to seek reality in just such a case as this.

So at the outset I went to the Library of Congress and studied the decision and the briefs for the parties. I observed the names of the individuals and organizations who wrote these briefs. I went to other rooms of the library and read the citations in the footnotes to the court's decision and observed the names of the individuals and organizations who wrote these. That the great majority had a special self-interest was clear—that the Attorney General had made any effort to present anything other than their environmentalist propaganda was not. A letter to the Attorney General, asking why, seemed thoroughly justified.

However, another important step remained to be taken before the justification was complete. My studies in science had taught me that observation and experience are valuable tools in discerning truth, but often fallible. Memory is also fallible. I knew what my observation and experience had been in racial matters and I remembered my earlier readings in this field and several more recent studies. But the argument that "modern" anthropology had exploded observation, experience and all past research required serious review.

Accordingly I began reading again in the Boas school of anthropology. Boas, I knew, was considered the founder of the modern vogue, and I deliberately began studying his books before learning, from people who had known him over many years, the facts about Franz Boas himself—his minority group background, his arrival from Germany in 1886, his association with Columbia in 1896, his earlier non-equalitarian views on race, his change of heart in the late 1920s (the date will have significance later), the names of his students—Herskovits, Klineberg, Ashley Montagu—the nature of his department at Columbia, the influence in it of an instructor named Weltfish who later publicly announced that she had evidence to prove that the United States had used germ warfare in Korea,[1] and the reorganization of the department by Ralph Linton who was brought in from Wisconsin after Boas died. Linton dismissed all of Boas' appointees who had no tenure and Columbia finally dropped Weltfish on a charge of "too-long" tenure.

I read Boas before learning these things because I wanted to approach his ideas with an impartial mind, on their merits and not on the merits or demerits of the author. Yet page by page my amazement grew. Here was clever and insidious propaganda posing in the name of science, fruitless efforts at proof of unprovable theories, which I would be only too glad to point out to the Attorney General. I went on to Herskovits and others until the pattern began to repeat itself, the slippery techniques in evading the main issues, the prolix diversions, the sound without the substance. Was it possible that a

[1] Concerning some of Gene Weltfish's other activities, the March 15, 1951, edition of the Communist *Daily Worker* lists her as a sponsor of the American Peace Crusade. This organization has been cited by the Attorney General of the United States as subversive. The April 4, 1951, edition of the *Daily Worker* records her as one of the sponsors of the American Committee for the Protection of the Foreign Born. This Committee has also been cited by the Attorney General as subversive.

whole generation of Americans had been taken in by such writing as this? My wife and I began to read seriously and earnestly—after a few evenings we found ourselves laughing out loud.

Still I was not satisfied. Surely there must be some explanation. It was hardly possible that schools were being closed in Virginia, men threatened with jail in Ohio, on the basis of a hoax as transparent as this. Were there no professional scientists in America who saw what I saw?

And so I took the third step in the preliminaries to my letter to the Attorney General. By mail, by telephone, and finally by personal visits, North and South, I found professional scientists aplenty who saw what I saw. And I discovered something else. One prize-winning Northern scientist whom I visited at his home in a Northern city asked me, after I had been seated a few minutes in his living room, whether I was sure I had not been followed. Another disclosed in the privacy of his study that he had evidence he was being checked by mulattoes at his lectures. All, when first approached, were hesitant, withdrawn and fearful, and the reason was not far to seek. Their employers on whom their livelihood depended—the universities, the museums, the foundations—were either controlled by equalitarians or were intimidated by the race taboo. The scientists whom these institutions employed, if they were ever to hint at the truth, must do so deviously, under wraps over wraps, half seeming to say the opposite.

But as they grew to know me they gave me the facts without varnish. In long conversations and letters they provided the confirmation I needed. Many were internationally known. Some had received the highest prizes. Any public official who will guarantee their livelihood can get their names from me, on one condition—that the scientists themselves agree.

I do not hold a brief for or against the attitude of these men. Most of them expressed their reluctance in terms of a temporary condition. One was about to publish a book and he felt it more important in the long run to keep the track clear for the book than to declare his position now. Another had a confidential assignment for his state that he must first perform. Another said, "I cannot commit academic suicide. I still have work to do. But when I retire—!" Another was simply "biding his time." How much of this was rationalization, arising from a timidity that ought to be overcome, I would not venture to say. It was easy enough for me, a man entirely independent of control, to speak—indeed it made my obligation unavoidable. It was less easy for them.

A second element in the situation soon dawned on me. The difficulty was compounding itself. The South instinctively saw the real issue, yet it had been told so often that what it saw did not exist that it had almost come to believe it. In this respect the South was in an identical trance with the North but, as happens in such cases, it could not actually be brought to destroy itself. It fought the trance with a counter-illusion. It clung to the hope that the Constitution could save it—that states' rights was its best defense. I was soon to learn how profound this counter-illusion was. From governors to lawyers in the street I received the same despairing protest—"What else is left?" There seemed to be an agreement among public officials that race should no longer even be mentioned. Among the few Northern defenders of the South the same defeatism existed. Feverish talk about the validity of the 14th Amendment went on, up North, down South, while no one challenged the assumption at the root of the whole trouble—the validity of Boas.

I knew by now that this root, this hidden issue, would be more difficult to present than the issues in my letter to the President. The problem was complicated by several factors. One lay in the emotional echo in the intra-racial sphere of any discussion of innate limitations in the inter-racial sphere. Another was the existence of the mixed-blood who moved in the twilight zone between white and black and whom the equalitarian could present, in appearance and in scientific tests, as the object of discussion.

That there was some mixture everywhere in the United States was probable; that there was more in the North than in the South was certain, for the whiter the mixture the more frequent the northward migration. The thinking of Northerners was thus constantly exposed to a subtle deception—judgments were being made, so to speak, on half the evidence. Ordinarily, if one wished to analyze a substance, one did not mix it with other substances—one sought as pure a specimen as possible. To approach this condition with the Negro one had to leave the North and travel South, or better to Haiti, or better still to central Africa. There the essence could be observed, and judgment could be made as to how much—or how little—of this essence one wanted in one's descendants, whether the absorption was from the fountain head, or from sources already in stages of dilution. But the average Northerner had no opportunity for such evaluations.

Then there was the problem of human nature. White Southerners understood the Negro and in large measure loved him. They realized that the agitation rending the South originated with organized white minorities in conjunction with mixed-bloods well over on the white side of the spectrum. They deplored the deterioration this agitation was producing in existing race relations in the blacker South. Yet they could scarcely bring themselves to hurt their own. The South, after generations of experience, had developed customs and a way of life with the Negro that took his limitations into consideration with a minimum of friction and a maximum of kindness. It was entirely against these customs, these adaptations, openly to analyze and publicize the reasons for them. The issue was complicated enough without bearing the additional weight of this responsibility.

Or so it must have seemed. Again I held no brief against the leadership of the South. With their anthropologists silenced, and their consciences misled, they were indeed in a dilemma. I could not but believe that so far as it lay within my powers my purpose should be to embolden their anthropologists and relieve their consciences. The next step now was to put the situation as I saw it before the Attorney General—to test both fact and theory, science and law, against the minds of the Department of Justice. I had received only a perfunctory acknowledgment of my letter to the President. Perhaps the Attorney General would be in a better position to discuss the subject. Accordingly on March 16, 1959, five months after my letter to President Eisenhower, I addressed Mr. Rogers in these words:

Following my correspondence with your Department in December, I have had a chance to review your briefs in the school desegregation cases and also to scan, as carefully as time permitted, the nine relevant volumes of the *Supreme Court's Records and Briefs.* I hesitate to impose further upon your kindness, but my survey has left one question in my mind upon which the record does not appear to touch, and which you may be able to answer.

I turn to you for the reason that, as a non-adversary party to these proceedings, I understand you to have represented the people of the United States. Since a majority of the population of the South are obviously against integration, and since the Gallup Poll for September 24, 1958, indicates that 58% of the white population of the North would not put their children in schools where more than half the enrollment is Negro, it becomes a close question whether the decision of the Supreme Court in these cases was not in fact contrary to the wishes of a national majority. While I recognize that this would in no way affect the validity of the decision, it would seem to have placed a peculiar responsibility upon you.

The matter which I find curious is the omission in your briefs of any challenge to the authorities cited by the Court in Footnote 11 to their opinion of May 17, 1954. I assume there must have been some indication, in argument or elsewhere, that these authorities were to be used. They appear, in large measure, to form the foundation of the decision. They reflect a point of view rooted in what I may call modern equalitarian anthropology — a school which holds that all races are currently equal in their capacity for culture, and that existing inequalities of status are due solely to inequalities of opportunity. While the briefs for the State of Virginia touch upon the qualifications of some of the individual psychologists who testified in the lower courts, they contain no examination of the underlying anthropological theory. It seems to me that such an examination should have been made. I have a science degree, I have read with some diligence in the field of anthropology and I have discussed the subject with competent anthropologists. It is my considered opinion that two generations of Americans have been victimized by a pseudo-scientific hoax in this field, that this hoax is part of an equalitarian propaganda typical of the left-wing overdrift of our times, and that it will not stand an informed judicial test. I do not believe that ever before has science been more warped by a self-serving few to the deception and injury of so many. On this subject there may be disagreement. But it is clear to me the Court should have been invited to examine the question.

Allow me to give my reasons for this opinion. The Court says in Footnote 11 "See generally Myrdal, *An American Dilemma,*" and I start with this book. I need hardly dwell upon the highly socialistic bias of its foreign author, and the startling remarks with which his text is peppered, such as his comment that the American Constitution "is in many respects impractical and ill-suited for modern conditions," that the Constitutional Convention of 1787 "was nearly a plot against the common people" and that in the conflict between liberty and equality in the United States "equality is slowly winning." A foreign socialist could not, perhaps, have realized that Jefferson's statement "all men are created equal" was a corruption from the Virginia Declaration of Rights, where the original wording read "all men are created equally free," nor that if equality (in any sense other than equality of opportunity and equality before the law) is defeating liberty in the United States, then everything America has stood for is in jeopardy, but certainly it was essential that these matters be called to the Court's attention in evaluating Myrdal's book.

I hasten, however, to the basic hypothesis underlying Myrdal's 1400 pages. On pages 90-91 he introduces the doctrines of Franz Boas, a foreign-born Columbia University professor who arrived in the United States in 1886, who was himself a member of a racial minority group, and who may be called the father of equalitarian anthropology in America. From these pages forward, Myrdal's *Dilemma* is founded upon the philosophy of Boas and his disciples. Thereafter, one constantly finds in Myrdal such sentences as these:

"The last two or three decades have seen a veritable revolution in scientific thought on the racial characteristics of the Negro. . . . By inventing and applying ingenious specialized research methods, the popular race dogma [that races are not by nature equal in their capacity for culture] is being victoriously pursued into every corner and effectively exposed as fallacious or at least unsubstantiated. . . . It is now becoming difficult for even popular writers to express other views than the ones of racial equalitarianism and still retain intellectual respect."

If you have not already read him, I invite you to a thorough and impartial study of Boas. I am confident you will find his views wholly unconvincing, his doctrines more "unsubstantiated" than those he attacks, and his approach so saturated with wishful thinking as to be pathetic. In even the most superficial analysis of the subject, Boas should have been challenged and his more obvious errors exposed. Boas, for example, may have been convinced that the average African's improvident indifference to "tomorrow" is just a healthy "optimism", but I dare say the proverbial reasonable man on a jury would think of it less charitably.

If the deceptions of the Boas school were unconscious, they were nevertheless serious. People, for instance, were induced to believe that because early anthropologists put emphasis on brain pan size in their studies of race, and brain pan size later proved to be an invalid criterion, this automatically made all races equal. No one took the time to point out that not only is brain pan size not a final test of intelligence, but that, even if it were, equal brain size would not prove equal capacity for civilization. The character-intelligence index—the combination of intelligence with all of the qualities that go under the name of character, including especially the willingness to resist rather than to appease evil—forms the only possible index of the capacity for civilization as Western Europeans know it, and there is no test for this index save in observing the native culture in which it results. Such observation does not sustain the doctrine of equality.

Indeed, the entire foundation of the Boas theory rests on sand. It is based on the assumption that present day cultural differences between the Negro and other races are due, not to any natural limitations, but to isolation and historical accident. This theme has been taken up again and again by later anthropologists such as Kluckhohn of Harvard, and repeated as established scientific fact. I may illustrate the argument by comparing the condition of the white tribes of Northern Europe just before the fall of Rome with the Negro tribes in the Congo. Both were primitive and barbaric, both were isolated from civilization. With the conquest of Rome by the white barbarians, the northern tribes were brought in contact with the ancient Greco-Roman civilization and gradually absorbed its culture. The Negro, on the other hand, lacked such a contact and therefore remained in *statu quo*.

This was Boas' historical accident, and his explanation of the Negro's present level of civilization in Africa. Boas had various additional points and refinements of his thesis, such as the advantage the white barbarians enjoyed in contiguity of habitat and the more moderate differences in modes of manufacture in earlier times, which made it easier for backward peoples in those days to compete commercially with more advanced cultures than was the case in later centuries when our white civilization invaded Africa, but these arguments hang on the first point. In other words, had the Negroes shown the enterprise and initiative of the white barbarians, the Negroes themselves would have established a contiguity of habitat and had the advantage of more moderate differences in modes of manufacture.

As far as isolation is concerned, it hardly seems necessary to point out that the Alps did not keep the white barbarians out of Italy, and that the Nile Valley was open to the Negroes into Egypt. One observer, recently returned from an intensive tour of Africa and himself apparently a racial equalitarian, nevertheless feels compelled to include these sentences in his report:

"Why, when in China, India, Mesopotamia and on the Mediterranean coasts and islands, men isolated almost completely from one another, during some 5,000 years independently developed writing and metal tools, invented compasses, built temples and bridges, formulated philosophies, wrote books and poems—why, then, did similar progress not occur in Africa?

"I posed the question to many Africans. Their answer: the desert, the heat, disease, isolation—and always these words: 'For centuries our most vigorous young men were taken off as slaves.'

"The answer falls short. China has a desert; India's climate is as hot and as unhealthy; Mesopotamia indeed is hotter—and was surrounded by deserts. As for the slave trade, why were the Africans not making slaves of the Portuguese and the Arabs?"

This report, prepared by the assistant to the publisher of "Time" magazine, goes on to seek justification for the equalitarian viewpoint in the modern intelligence test and the modern performance of the exceptional Negro, answers which fall as far short as the others. The field of the intelligence test, like the field of Boas' anthropology, is filled with wishful thinking, with comparisons of the better Negroes and the poorer whites, with studies of mulattoes whose successes are largely proportionate to the admixture of white genes, and with similar avoidance of the essential point, namely, that in matters of race either the average of one must be compared with the average of the other, or the best of one must be compared with the best of the other.

If we are to compare averages, there is probably no better laboratory than the rural area around Chatham, Ontario, Canada. Chatham is a town at the northern end of the pre-Civil War "underground railroad" where a community of the descendants of escaped slaves has existed for 100 years. The social and economic situation of Negroes and whites in the rural area around Chatham is approximately equal. The schools have always been integrated, yet the tests of Negroes in these rural schools show them, after 100 years, to be as far below the whites in the same schools as the Negroes in the schools of the South are below the whites in the schools of the South. Dr. H. A. Tanser, now Superintendent of Schools at Chatham, published a study of this matter in 1939. The study is never mentioned by the modern school of equalitarian anthropology, but you will find it in the Library of Congress. Did your Department give it consideration?

In this connection, you are perhaps aware that Dr. Audrey M. Shuey, Chairman of the Department of Psychology at Randolph-Macon Woman's College, published a report in 1958 surveying and summarizing the results of 40 years of intelligence tests involving whites and Negroes. Dr. Shuey took her B.A. at the University of Illinois, her M.A. at Wellesley, and her Ph.D. at Columbia. Her book contains a foreword by Dr. Henry E. Garrett, former president of the American Psychological Association, the Eastern Psychological Association, the New York State Association of Applied Psychology and the Psychometric Society. In his foreword, Dr. Garrett says:

"Dr. Shuey finds that at several age levels and under a variety of conditions, Negroes regularly score below whites. There is, to be sure, an overlapping of scores, a number of Negroes scoring above the white medians. This overlap means that many individual Negroes achieve high scores on the tests. But the mean differences persist.

Dr. Shuey concludes that the regularity and consistency of the results strongly imply a racial basis for these differences. I believe that the weight of evidence supports her conclusion."

Dr. Shuey states that "the remarkable consistency of test results . . . all point to the presence of some native differences between Negroes and whites determined by intelligence tests", and she adds the significant comment: "The tendency for the IQ's of colored children to become progressively lower with increase in age has been reported by a number of investigators who tested Negro children. . . . One is confronted with the probability of a continuance during adolescence of what seems to be a widening gap between the races." I recognize that Dr. Shuey's report was not extant at the time of the Brown decision, but a large part of her material was available, and in my opinion should have been submitted to the Court. I repeat that I do not consider the intelligence test decisive, as I believe character to be more important than intelligence, but in answer to those who use the intelligence test to support theories of racial equality, surely Tanser's and Shuey's material belonged in the record.

If, on the other hand, we compare the best with the best, the discrepancies are even clearer. I had occasion to ask Kluckhohn a question with respect to a statement in his *Mirror for Man* at page 126. This statement reads: "It is true that the total richness of Negro civilizations is *at least quantitatively* less impressive than that of Western or Chinese civilization." (Emphasis mine). I asked Kluckhohn if he would mind defining in what respects he found it *qualitatively* as impressive. I told him I was curious as to one poem equal to Milton's *Paradise Lost,* one history equal to Gibbon's *Decline and Fall,* one novel equal to Dickens' *David Copperfield,* one playwright equal to Shakespeare, one philosopher equal to Aristotle, one medical discovery equal to Salk's polio vaccine, one military leader equal to Napoleon, one inventor equal to Edison, one physicist equal to Einstein, one pioneer equal to Columbus, one statesman equal to Abraham Lincoln, one composer equal to Beethoven, one painter equal to Rembrandt. I have received no reply, but Kluckhohn's "at least quantitatively" seems to me typical of the deceptive words used by our modern equalitarian anthropology. The Court should not have been left in the dark on this tendency. Although they do not specifically cite Kluckhohn, he is one of the leaders of the modern school on which Myrdal rests his case.

I have found that a favorite method used by Boas and Kluckhohn for throwing dust in the eyes of the public is to create an impression that there is really no such thing as race. Although Kluckhohn begins the third paragraph of the fifth chapter of his *Mirror for Man* with the sentence "There are undoubtedly human races," he nevertheless entitles this chapter "Race: A Modern Myth." His thesis is that culture, not race, is what makes human beings what they are. Yet nowhere is the obvious fact examined that culture is absorbed, refined and advanced in proportion to racial capacity. There are, of course, certain modifying variables, among the chief of which are climate and economic conditions. The white culture of New England differs from the white culture of the Deep South, but not as much as the white culture of southern Florida differs from the black culture of Haiti, where the climate is approximately the same. That is to say, the effect of the variables is clearly less decisive than the fundamental difference in race.

Undoubtedly an individual or group, taken out of the cultural environment of their own race and brought up in that of another, will sometimes absorb some features of the culture of the new environment, but in such instances they become parasites upon the culture of the second race. They are carried up, or carried down, as the case may be, by the overwhelming impact of the environment of the second race. Their own capacity to contribute to, and to sustain, a culture can only be judged by the performance of their own race in its native habitat. And if that capacity is low, then too many of them, too freely integrated, must inevitably in the long run lower the culture of the second race.

There have, not unnaturally, been situations in which a race has captured the spark of culture in one habitat but not in another. In the case of the fall of the Roman Empire, the barbarians were, broadly speaking, members of the same race as the conquered. Here we find two branches of the white race, one of which had produced a culture while the other had not, and here the Boas theory of historical accident is tenable. Similarity of tinder permitted passage of the spark. It was still the white race that absorbed, and eventually carried forward, the Roman culture.

The essential question in this whole controversy is whether the Negro, given every conceivable help regardless of cost to the whites, is capable of full adaptation to our white civilization within a matter of a few generations, or whether the record indicates such adaptation cannot be expected save in terms of many hundreds, if not thousands, of years, and that complete integration of these races, especially in the heavy black belts of the South, can result only in a parasitic deterioration of white culture, with or without genocide. I am certain neither you nor the Court, nor any significant number of Northerners would knowingly shackle their racial brothers in the South against their will with a system which would produce either of the latter results. The sin of Cain would pale by comparison.

Yet to my mind it seems obvious that all the facts, and a preponderance of theory, are against Myrdal and his authorities. I would go so far as to say that in the last fifty years anthropology has been drafted to serve the demi-Goddess of Equalitarianism instead of the Goddess of Truth, and that the modern school in this field has a stern judgment to face, both at the bar of American public opinion and at the hands of two generations of youth whose thinking has been corrupted by it. One does not build a healthy society on error. One faces the truth, and deals with it as best one can.

I pass now from Myrdal, and the sources upon which his more general assumptions rest, to the remaining authorities cited in Footnote 11. All of these deal primarily with the adverse psychological effect of segregation upon Negroes and only secondarily with its alleged adverse effect upon white children. Nowhere is any study cited of a third question, namely, of the quite possible adverse effect of *integration* upon whites in schools with large percentages of Negroes. Was any such study made and presented to the Court?

The third question was well put by William Polk in his book *Southern Accent*: "If the Negro is entitled to lift himself up by enforced association with the white man, why should not the white man be entitled to prevent himself from being pulled down by enforced association with the Negro?" This question seems particularly important in view of the patent partiality of the authorities cited in favor of integration. The majority of these appear either to belong to Negro or other minority groups, or to have prepared their studies under the auspices of such groups. To expect these groups to present impartial reports on the subject of racial discrimination is like expecting a saloon keeper to prepare an impartial study on prohibition, or a meat packer to pass an unbiased judgment on the Humane Slaughter Bill. Their point of view is important and deserves consideration. Many of them are brilliant and consecrated men. But to permit them to provide the overwhelming preponderance of the evidence is manifestly not justice. If this is compounded by an absence of any consideration of the damaging effects of integration upon white children, it becomes doubly serious. While the brief for the State of Virginia touches upon the subject, it seems to me that the people of the United States, whom you represented, had a particular interest in seeing it more fully developed. I would appreciate your directing me to such a study, if one was made, and also your providing me with some explanation as to why the evidence on damage to the Negro was from such partisan sources.

Any American worthy of the name feels an obligation of kindness and justice toward his fellow man. He is willing to give every individual his chance, whatever his race, but in those circumstances where a race must be dealt with as a race, he realizes that the level of the average must be controlling, and that the relatively minor handicap upon the superior individual of the segregated race, if it be a handicap at all, must be accepted until the average has reached the point where desire for association is mutual.

This leads me to my final query. I will be frank to say that I was startled at the uncritical manner in which the Supreme Court was allowed to accept one phrase in the language of the lower court, to wit: "A sense of inferiority [produced by segregation] affects the motivation of a child to learn." Did neither you nor counsel for any of the appellees take occasion to point out that if a child is by nature inferior, enforced association with his superiors will increase his realization of his inferiority, while if he is by nature not inferior, any implication of inferiority in segregation, if such there be, will only serve as a spur to greater effort? Throughout history, challenges of this sort, acting upon individuals, groups and races of natural capacity, have proved a whip to achievement, times without number. The point was one of the legal hinges on which the case turned. In fact without it the decision falls apart, for there is no other even remotely arguable excuse why separate facilities cannot be made equal within any possible stretch of the meaning of the Fourteenth Amendment. Consequently, I would have thought it imperative that you raise it.

Copies of this letter were sent to the President and to each member of the Supreme Court. I had no answer or acknowledgment from the Attorney General. Two members of the Supreme Court acknowledged receipt, which was all they properly could do. No other acknowledgments were received.

Silence, of course, was an answer of a sort. It settled any doubts in my mind concerning the attitude of the Attorney General. As to the secondary purpose of the letter, its usefulness as a tool in simplifying my correspondence, this hope was soon dispelled. "The Second Putnam Letter", as it came to be called, involved me in controversy as lengthy as the first.

I chose the Charleston, South Carolina, *News and Courier*, the South's oldest daily, to launch the text, and its distinguished editor, Thomas R. Waring, printed it in full on March 22. He was also kind enough to say editorially:

"Mr. Putnam has ample grounds for labelling the psychological and anthropological theories on which the Supreme Court wrote its racial decisions as a scientific hoax. The label is long delayed, but we believe it will stick. Though psychologists whose studies have tended to show up racial differences in intelligence have met with varying degrees of suppression, the facts are beginning to be recognized.

"Even more important than relative intelligence is character and responsibility. Mr. Putnam brings out this racial difference with kindness but vigor. Competent leaders of the Negro race should not reject these facts on account of emotionalism but should adapt them to their own racial problems. Surely the numerous Negroes who have surmounted handicaps must realize that more is involved in the march from jungle to industrial civilization than calories and classrooms.

"Centuries in the history of mankind cannot be changed in a generation or two. The colored people who languished thousands of years in Africa have blossomed faster than any people on earth in the freedom of the United States. Most of them have made this progress in the South. They can destroy it by heedless insistence on too much too fast.

"Carleton Putnam is doing a favor to colored as well as white Americans by focusing light on the truth."

As Dabney had done with my letter to the President, Waring made up tear sheets containing both the letter and the editorial and sent them to 1700 newspaper editors in the United States. In spite of its greater length and complexity it was again widely reprinted with favorable comment throughout the South, and totally ignored in the North.

However, enough copies reached the North by private mailings from Southerners to produce a selective reaction. Northerners who had had time to think about the hidden issue sent me enthusiastic letters and telegrams. Equalitarian college professors were scornful in a way that seemed to mask a great uneasiness. Nor was it long before the National Association for the Advancement of Colored People was heard from—not directly, but through Southern editors who forwarded to me the letters they received from the Association.

I preferred to be direct. I wrote the Association inviting detailed criticism of my stand and relished the exchange which followed. Having had no answer from Rogers, I was eager to test every point I had made against the knowledge of others who were involved in the school decision, whether these minds were members of the NAACP or high on the faculties of universities.

Indeed, an official of the NAACP, a grandson of a slave, wrote the best critique, in style and tone, of any I received. I say it with sadness, for every argument he advanced I was obliged to refute. I told this official I wanted to make clear that I was addressing him not as an individual but as a symbol of an organization, some of whose objectives I believed to be wrong and against whose aggressions my race was being forced to defend itself. Then I took his points and dealt with them individually. Each of them appears in the next chapter of this book.

I followed the same procedure in the case of the college professors. But in this instance I was puzzled at the deliberate casuistry and the effort to draw attention from the main point by verbose irrelevancies. At the start of an exchange these gentlemen were sometimes swaggering. The head of the anthropology department at an Ivy League university replied to a courteous request for criticism as follows: "They [Southerners] seem bent on demonstrating their intellectual inferiority to the Negro by such performances as yours. Why don't you prove your boast of superior intelligence by showing some of it?" This scholarly comment concluded a letter which failed to meet a single issue on its merits. I was regretfully obliged to reply in kind: "My conviction grows daily that none of your group can support with solid fact a single one of your equalitarian contentions, and that consciously or unconsciously you have victimized two entire generations of students. The sooner you are brought to the bar of public opinion to account for this hoax the better. . . . You have undoubtedly intimidated for the time being a number of your colleagues, but your day of accounting may be closer than you think."

Another swashbuckler, at another Ivy League university, began with a tone of patronizing ridicule. He questioned certain of my statements, demanded proof, and when the proof was supplied, changed the subject. When he was exposed there, he tried something else. The evasions were transparent and futile, and in the end the swashbuckler's tone had been converted to a plaintive respect. Concluding this exchange I was compelled to remark: "Your letter of December 28 is so lacking in intellectual integrity, so full of either deliberate or incredibly careless falsifications, that I am thoroughly alarmed."

Indeed, I trust my indignation in this case does not conceal the sincerity of my feeling. I was frankly astonished at the level of intellectual character in academic circles betrayed by this phase of my correspondence.

I was equally concerned by what seemed to be a complete emotional block in the minds of certain readers when it came to facing the hidden issue at all. The problem was particularly noticeable in dealing with people I knew personally. They begged me not to raise the subject, or felt it wiser to agree to disagree, or wished to keep our friendship undisturbed by argument. There was a uniform unwillingness in this group to examine the matter logically, yet, as I have said, they were often the quickest to turn the equalitarian charge of emotionalism against me. To make these people think seemed impossible.

Unfortunately they constituted a very large percentage of the younger generation in the North, educated since the social revolution of 1932. I wondered whether perhaps they were reluctant to examine this latest consequence of the equalitarian ideology for fear of what the examination might mean in terms of other concepts. They were companioned in their blindness by the sociologists, calling themselves social "scientists", who were often older and had been among the professional liberals who sponsored the original overdrift. These men were in no way qualified themselves to be dogmatic upon questions of physical anthropology, zoology or genetics, yet they closed their minds to any discussion in these fields which might invalidate the structure they had built upon the equalitarian foundation. These men were paying the immemorial penalty of deceit, they had hypnotized others so long they were now the victims of their own trance. Their favorite opening gambit was "No educated man believes any longer . . ," to which they were accustomed to receive no challenge whatever. When they heard instead, "Let's see about that," I observed a scurrying for the intellectual exits.

But, all in all, I profited from the debate, whether verbal or written, took the measure of the equalitarian position, observed their arguments and their rebuttals, and learned something of the manner in which they seduced the unwary mind. Either from their silences or their comments, I had or sensed the thinking of Kluckhohn and Handlin of Harvard, Murdock of Yale, Herskovits of Northwestern, and Fosdick of Union Theological Seminary. There were dozens of others, from Richard Nixon to Eleanor Roosevelt, from Nelson Rockefeller to Billy Graham, from Allan Nevins to Ralph McGill. To all the arguments I received, I gave the most earnest thought. If I were wrong, I wanted to know it, and to know why.

In the end, the silences proved nothing, and the arguments nothing. And the reader has the right to know why.

CHAPTER III

POINT BY POINT

It was finally obvious that there could be no answer to this challenge save in getting down to cases. My second letter had in itself raised new questions in many minds and had stung the integrationists to new propaganda. Moreover, there were the old issues that kept recurring in my mail, either on the fringes of the hidden issue or in totally different spheres. Their aspects were so manifold that no connected narrative could encompass them. The most succinct and realistic method of treatment seemed to be the format in which they themselves reached me—as a question, often rhetorical it is true, often ending in an exclamation point rather than a question mark, but in a staccato pitch inviting a staccato reply.

Since there were many questions, on many points, which were repetitive, I began going through the accumulated letters, winnowing out the duplications, until I had a residue of material that appeared representative of the mass as a whole. The points in these I classified, using the major categories the debate had produced, and then proceeded to answer them as concisely as possible.

My plan at first was to use the result solely for private circulation, printed as a pamphlet and mailed to each correspondent. But in the course of preparation I found myself sending both the questions and answers to experts in their respective fields—to anthropologists, judges, ministers, editors and politicians—asking their comments, and in the process a demand arose for publication in book form. Both Northerners and Southerners appealed to the Birmingham Committee and to me for copies in quantity, with the suggestion that the two letters be included between the same covers. The latter proposal had a special advantage as it made unnecessary a re-statement of the earlier material and presented the background from which the questions sprang.

This book is sufficient witness that I yielded to the suggestion. Let me assure the reader that I have kept an open mind, and an open manuscript, to the last minute to receive any data that might significantly change any point in my replies or bring new questions to bear upon the issues. There has been nothing static about the following section, and after it has gone to press I am sure additional questions will arrive which I will wish had reached me sooner.

Anthropology and Intermarriage

I am a Negro. Your letter to the President was a pretty hard slap in the face for me. Can't you realize how it feels to be colored, and to read something like that in a newspaper?

No one wants to slap anybody in the face less than I do. I am totally out of sympathy with those who show discourtesy to you or any other racial group, any time, anywhere. I will never hurt another man's feelings if I can help it, and I believe that the greatest of all human qualities is the ability to put one's self in the other person's place.

Therefore, I regret beyond words the necessity for writing as I did. But in this case your leaders have left me, and other members of my race who have studied the question, no choice. Your leaders were the aggressors. I have had word from many colored people agreeing with my position and with what I say to you now.

Your leaders were not content with the progress being made by mutual agreement and understanding throughout the South. They had to take more by force. Under such circumstances you cannot expect me, or any white man who perceives the real issue, to keep silent.

The truth is that responsible Southerners have deliberately weakened their own defense because of their unwillingness to raise the underlying problem. They talk of states' rights when they should be talking anthropology, and they do so out of instinctive human kindness. I fear the time has come when they can afford this kindness no longer. There is a point at which kindness imposed upon ceases to be a virtue.

You and I do not see things from the same point of view. We disagree on fundamentals. Therefore, isn't it best to avoid arguments?

No, because it is the fundamentals that I want to examine.

The North had to force the South to give up slavery. Why should not the North force the South to integrate?

Morally the two situations are diametrically opposite. While some Northerners made fortunes out of the slave trade, relatively few owned slaves at the time of the Civil War and consequently they could, with some justification, demand that the South be equally virtuous. But very few Northerners are in a position where they need put their children in schools with large percentages of Negroes. In forcing integration upon the South, the North is demanding that the South do what the North itself in similar circumstances would not do. It is an established fact that white people favor integration throughout the United States exactly in proportion as they do not need to practice it.

Are there any good reasons why Southern white children shouldn't be made to go to school with Negroes?

There are several, among them the fact that their parents don't want them to, but I will suggest the fundamental reason.

There is no basis in sound science for the assumption, promoted by various minority groups in recent decades, that all races are biologically equal in their capacity to advance, or even to sustain, what is commonly called Western civilization. They most emphatically are not.

The Negro race has various and valuable qualities. In those great attributes of the heart—sympathy and kindness—and in a sense of humor—the average[1] Negro, taken as an individual, is fully on a par with the average white. In certain skills the Negro ranks above the white. If I were lost in an African jungle my life might depend on the talents of a Negro. In other qualities of mind and character, qualities specially involved in our Western civilization, the full-blooded Negro is congenitally only partially adaptable. Hereafter, when I use such words as "inferior", "backward", and "unequal", I use them in this limited sense only.

---

1. While scientists dislike the concept suggested by the word "average", preferring the concept of "frequency", I have used "average" throughout this book as more understandable to the layman and equally acceptable in the context in which I employ it. For example, where a scientist would say the *frequency* with which emotionalism occurs in Negroes is greater than the *frequency* with which it occurs in whites, I would say the *average* Negro is more emotional than the *average* white.

Such being our understanding, let me state the situation in its simplest terms, quoting a letter to me from a Professor of Physiology in one of our leading medical schools: "School integration is social integration, and social integration means an ever increasing rate of interbreeding. [This is true regardless of whether the sexes are separated in schools. Little brother would still bring his new Negro friend home after school.] As a biologist I see the process as a mixing of Negro genes in our white germ plasm, a process from which there can be no unmixing."

Some disagreement may exist as to the extent to which the admixture of Negro genes has affected white civilizations in the past. I have never anywhere seen the claim that it did the white race any good. Consider the history of the West Indies and other Latin American countries. But in any case, we are left with the query, what great civilization of the kind we are seeking to develop in the West ever arose *after* an admixture of Negro genes?

Since the question answers itself, I must ask the Northern integrationist by what authority he claims the right to gamble with the white civilization of the South, against the will of its people, while he personally sits secure with his children in all white schools, or in schools with negligible percentages of Negroes.

To me this appears as one of the worst examples of hypocrisy and brutality in all history. However, it differs only in degree from a related trend of our times. It is always easy and sometimes justifiable to spend the money that someone else has earned—a principle which the equalitarians understand thoroughly. It is equally easy and never justifiable to spend someone else's children.

Are there enough Negroes in the United States to make any real difference if we absorb them?

The ratio of non-whites to whites in the United States as a whole in the 1950 census was around 10%. If completely absorbed, this would be a substantial admixture, with noticeable effects. More serious is the fact that a large part of the Negro population is concentrated in the South. In 1950, Mississippi had 46%, South Carolina 39%, Louisiana 33%, Alabama 32%, and Georgia 31% non-whites. Absorption in any of these states would be disastrous. It would be almost as bad in any other southern state. There are

131 counties in nine southern states in which the Negro population exceeds the white.

Is there any evidence that the Negro really cares about intermarriage with the white race?

Scan the Negro press. Here, as an example, is a quotation from the Pittsburgh *Courier,* a leading Negro weekly, for August 15, 1959:

"The Negro phobes and crackerologists are ever shouting warnings that this or that lowering of racial barriers will lead inevitably to inter-marriage and intermixture. Well, I say that's just fine and exactly what this nation needs to maintain its world supremacy . . . We live in an unwholesome clandestine atmosphere in which we whisper of healthy love and desires across the color line but fear to speak out boldly. . . .

"Every community worth its salt should have a frankly interracial club or association where the boys and gals, colored and white, could associate, drink and dance . . . Of course we favor racial mixing, including marriage, and are working openly to kill all racially restrictive legislation and social segregation and discrimination."

I have before me a copy of the Negro magazine *Ebony* for February, 1960. On page 66 there is a picture of a Negro next to a picture of a white girl. Under the picture of the Negro is the following caption: "Hebrew Holy charm around Sammy's neck is gift from Eddie Cantor. Planning to marry Canadian blonde, Sammy says: 'The Bible says "Take unto yourself a wife." And it don't say nothing about her color.' "

May I also quote an interview with Congressman Adam Clayton Powell appearing in *United States News and World Report* on September 5, 1952:

"Q. What is the attitude of the Negro in the United States on the subject of intermarriage? Is it discussed frequently in the press?

"A. Yes, but on an objective basis. In fact, an increasingly large number of Negro leaders are marrying whites of extremely stable and respected families.

"Q. Is there much more fraternizing in the Northern cities between Negroes and whites, especially in the large Negro centers like Harlem, than there used to be?

"A. Yes, much more.

"Q. Is there any tendency among the Negroes to reject that, or are they welcoming it?

"A. They are very definitely welcoming it. An increasing number of fine leaders on both sides are marrying.

"Q. What is the argument that is used by Negro leaders in answer to the point that is sometimes made that, if intermarriages continue in the next 25 to 30 years, then the races will be adulterated somewhat as they are in Cuba and Brazil?

"A. I have heard that argument, but it doesn't amount to any argument at all from my standpoint, because if we are fighting for integration, well then there it is. I mean, you can't fight against segregation and want separation. We must be consistent.

"Q. I'm not sure that that is clear.

"A. The Negro leaders are fighting against segregation. Therefore, they can't have a position on the one hand against segregation and on the other hand against inter-racial marriage."

My Harvard professor claims that miscegenation increases when one race is kept inferior to another and that anything that increases the equality of the two races minimizes the opportunities for miscegenation. Is not this true?

It depends in what sense one uses the word "miscegenation". Your professor is using it in the sense of illicit intercourse. It is manifestly not true that keeping a race inferior increases the rate of legalized marriage with the intent to bear and rear children which is the basic question at issue in the integration fight. In illicit connections every effort is made to avoid breeding. When social integration occurs, this sort of "equality" invites legalized unions in which breeding is a major object.

Even if illegal unions resulted in offspring as numerous as do marriages, the social consequences would still be quite different. When white men marry Negro women in any numbers the trend is toward a gradual change in social attitudes of acceptance, and a slow infiltration of the dominant white society by the offspring, with the consequent changing of the standards of that society, as evidenced in various Latin American countries.

On the other hand when white men have illicit intercourse with

Negro women, not only are offspring avoided if possible but, if offspring do result, the latter are isolated from the dominant white society and consequently do not have any comparable chance to change its standards, as heretofore evidenced in the United States.

While there is no positive scientific proof that the Negro is the equal of the white man, neither is there any positive scientific proof that he is not. Under these circumstances, how can the Negro's inferiority be assumed?

It is true that anthropology is not an exact science in the sense that mathematics is, and that its propositions cannot be proved or disproved like mathematical formulae. Nevertheless, the evidence is as clear as the nature of the science permits, and it is all that reasonable men can ask.

In the management of human affairs, all law and all practical judgments are based on a balance of probabilities. In our civil courts, decisions are reached on probabilities alone. In the criminal law, the balance of probabilities must reach the extent of being "beyond a reasonable doubt", but can seldom amount to a certainty.

In applying the findings of a science like anthropology to our daily lives, the same principles must govern, and I will go so far as to say that not only does the evidence on the incomplete adaptability of the Negro meet the requirements of the civil law, it meets those of the criminal law. Observation and experience confirm it "beyond a reasonable doubt".

A northern psychologist, commenting upon the above answer, remarks that in his opinion a thorough study of Negro-white intelligence tests *does* reveal conclusive mathematical proof of the Negro's limitations. To my mind, the point is academic. But to those interested, I not only recommend a reading of Dr. Shuey's[2] and Dr. Tanser's books cited in my letter to the Attorney General, but also "A Scientist's Report on Race Differences", by Dr. Frank C. J. McGurk appearing in the September 21, 1956 edition of *U. S. News and World Report,* as well as " 'Negro vs White Intelligence'—

2. A review in the English publication *The Eugenics Review* for October 1960 calls Dr. Shuey's book, *The Testing of Negro Intelligence* (1958), "as impartial a study as any that have been made in the racial field."

An Answer", by the same author, in the winter, 1959, issue of the *Harvard Educational Review.*

While, as I have suggested elsewhere, skull criteria as applied to racial differences are in a state of flux owing to research presently in progress by such men as Wilder Pennfield of McGill University, there is no question that the frontal lobes of the typical Negro are smaller and the cerebral cortex less wrinkled than the typical white's. For an excellent study in this regard, see Cornelius J. Connolly, *The External Morphology of the Primate Brain,* 1950. Connolly has pointed out very significant differences between Caucasoid and American Negro brains, particularly in the sulci of the cortical frontal lobes, an area decisive to higher intelligence. Ward C. Halstead's *Brain and Intelligence,* 1947, considers the relation of these lobes to control over the emotions and to judgment. I deal further with questions of documentation in footnote 7, and specifically with the frontal lobes on pages 53-54.

You have spoken of white civilizations being pulled down by the admixture of Negro genes. How can you prove this?

I will answer the question by asking another. Can anyone name one stable republic in all history that was predominantly, or even substantially, Negro? The capacity for a free civilization involves many attributes, self-control (which, among other things, includes resistance to emotionalism), self-reliance, self-responsibility, willingness to bear the burdens of others without casting upon others the burdens one should bear one's self, willingness both to accept the verdict of majorities and to concede the rights of minorities, willingness to obey the law even when it hurts, willingness to support rather than to raid a treasury, emphasis upon the importance of the individual. Our American Republic, with all its faults, is, together with England, the fine flower of centuries of self-discipline and experience in free government by the English speaking branch of the white race. I will not say no other branch, but I will say few other races, have ever approached this achievement, least of all the Negro.

My answer covers the sphere of government alone. I have dealt elsewhere with the Negro in relation to other aspects of our culture.

Are not many individual Negroes superior to many individual whites?

Here again we have the point that I made in my letter to the Attorney General: In dealing with matters of race, we must either compare average with average or best with best; we cannot logically compare best with worst.

When the chart of the Caucasoid race as a whole is laid beside the chart of the Negro race as a whole, in those attributes involved in our type of civilization, the Caucasoid will be found superior at each level except perhaps the lowest where the question arises, can one be better at being bad?

I am reminded here of one man who wrote me ridiculing the reference in my letter to the President to a Negro settlement in Africa and asking, "why not point to the whites in Hog Wallow, Arkansas?" The answer, of course, must be that the settlement in Africa is typical of the best that the Negro, *left on his own resources,* can produce while Hog Wallow, Arkansas, is not typical of the best, or even of the average, for the white race.

If some Negroes contribute more to our civilization than some whites, why then should we not sort people by worth rather than by race?

In all the ordinary judgments of life, in dealings between individuals, we should. But in those matters which involve social association, and hence the possibility of intermarrying, the element of race inevitably enters because each individual carries in his genes the heritage of his race and this will be passed on in the breeding process. As one Southerner put the point: "However weak the individual white man, his ancestors produced the greatness of Europe; however strong the individual black, his ancestors never lifted themselves from the darkness of Africa."

Were there not magnificent Negro civilizations in Africa when white men were drinking blood out of skulls? What about Timbuktu?

To begin with, I know of no period when white men drank blood out of skulls. Secondly, if one searched through all history for the time when the best pure Negro culture, uninfluenced by white help, was at its peak, and then sought the time when the worst pure white culture was at its bottom, I suppose one might decide that, as a white man, one would have preferred to have lived among the Negroes, although I doubt it. I have not heard of any tribal poetry among Negroes comparable to Beowulf or the Nibelungenlied. In any case the same point about comparing best with worst applies here as applied in my answer to the question on page 42.

Of greater importance, it would be well to examine more closely these so-called "magnificent Negro civilizations" in Africa. At one time, and a very brief one, there were west Sudan kingdoms with more brilliance than the contemporary ones in, say, Scandinavia, but they could not be compared with the contemporary Byzantine Empire or even the troubadour civilization of Provence.

As for the city of Timbuktu, can you mention the Arab-inspired Mosque school of that city in the same breath with the University of Paris, also founded in the twelfth century? Which of their medieval professors has the modern influence of St. Thomas Aquinas? Remember also that Timbuktu was ruled by an Arab nobility and a slightly colored Tuareg upper class. Full-blooded Negroes were at the bottom of the social scale.

Was there not once a great Negro Pharaoh on the throne of Egypt?

There was no black dynasty on the throne of Egypt as long as Egypt was Egypt in any real sense. The Nubian dynasty between 742-633 B.C. was a period of retrogression.

Although Nubia has always bounded Egypt on the south, and began absorbing some Caucasoid racial elements before the dawn of history, it has never contributed significantly to the culture of Egypt.

Does not Basil Davidson's "Lost Cities of Africa" prove the existence of ancient Negro civilizations?

Mr. Davidson is a romantic propagandist for the equalitarian ideology. His book breathes his passion to prove Negro equality into every line, the passion being more apparent that the proof.

Moreover, it is impossible to give credence to an author who can write a sentence such as the following: "That the chiefs and some of the tribes of the coasts were easily corrupted into wholesale slave trading is obvious enough: the step from domestic slavery, which they had always practiced, to the sale of slaves was all too easily made." This passage suggesting white corruption of African chiefs should be laid beside the known facts regarding the Yam Festival of the Ashanti Negroes. In this rite at the end of the first rainy season of each year, native slaves were herded into a compound and trussed up to stakes. The compound was surrounded by thorny plants. At a signal the black debutantes of the season were turned loose with knives to hack and bleed their way into the compound where they proceeded to cut the slaves to pieces. Indeed, students are of the opinion that, with the possible exception of the Aztec, the earth has never known a bloodier race than the African Negro.[3]

I may add that in 1960, as reported by international police circles, girl children are being captured in northwestern Nigeria, in the "democratic" modern state of Ghana, and sold into domestic slavery to westernized Negroes in Dahomey. It is reported by the same police organization that some of these children become the victims of human sacrifice cults, including cannibalism, and that the current, 1960, price is $825.

Mr. Davidson overlooks these matters when he speaks of black chiefs and tribes corrupted by whites. White hands were far from clean, but they were several shades cleaner than the black.[4] The pattern repeats itself. Invariably the equalitarian, or Marxist, will try to blame the better for the conduct of the worse.

Recorded history is only a small fragment on the total scale of time. Civilizations rise and fall. The British were primitives once, then rose. Why may not the Negroes do the same?

It is now generally believed that civilization, as distinguished from native culture, had its beginnings in one zone, in what is sometimes called the Fertile Crescent, and spread from there, as a fire spreads, to other areas of the earth, the only uncertain excep-

---

3. I spare the reader further details on this point. For those with strong stomachs who seek documentation I may mention *The Seething African Pot* (1936) by Daniel Thwaite; *The Mind of the Savage* (1929) by Raoul Allier; and *Mau Mau Man-Hunt* (1957) by William W. Baldwin. An informative short article by Joseph E. Evans may be found in the *Wall Street Journal* for August 23, 1960.

4. I do not consider here the good done by whites in Africa. See pages 77 and 80.

tion to this theory being the civilizations of Central America and Peru. Different races caught up the spark, so to speak, according to the quality of the tinder they themselves constituted, the Chinese developing in one way, Europe in another, with variations among the sub-groups.

But the Negro race has done comparatively little with it, although they have had repeated exposure to the flame, in Africa, in Europe and in the Western Hemisphere. The moment the support of other races is withdrawn, they retrogress, as in Haiti.

If it be argued that some day, a thousand years from now, some change may occur in the Negro which will change the quality of the tinder, I would not discount the possibility but it is plainly irrelevant to the present controversy. We cannot force integration upon the South today on the strength of something that may occur a thousand years hence.

Did not the British retrogress after the Roman legions were withdrawn?

The British Gallo-Romans maintained an excellent northern brand of Celtic-Latin civilization until they were overwhelmed by Teutons still in the Hallstattian Iron Age. The records of the ecclesiastical councils before the Anglo-Saxon-Jute invasion show as much cultivation as the contemporary ones in Italy.

One may also compare the legends of King Arthur in England with those of the Emperor Christophe in Haiti.

Is it not true that climate accounts for the Negro's deficiencies in Africa and that a better climate will correct these eventually?

There are two schools of thought on the relation of climate and the Negro, neither of which gives any support to the equalitarian. One school points out that Africa has the highest average altitude of any of the five continents. While some of it is tropical jungle and burning desert, much of it is temperate plateau. The Negro tribes of the plateau are no more advanced that those of the jungle. In fact, the hinterland of the Gulf of Guinea, from which most of our American Negroes came, has a healthier climate than many areas where white civilizations have thrived—and far healthier than the steaming rain jungles of Yucatan and Guatemala where the great Mayan civilization developed. Conversely, while the Mayans developed their astronomy and mathematics in Central America, the Algonquins achieved nothing in New England.

The second school maintains that climate operating on the Negro over thousands of years has produced many hereditary physical characteristics, such as sickle-cell anemia which gives the Negro his relative immunity to malaria, and that these characteristics have their parallel in the Negro psyche. In other words the tropics have conditioned the Negro in both mind and body to tropical life.

It will be clear at once that if nature has taken perhaps 30,000 years to adapt the Negro to the tropics, the qualities involved have become innate and cannot now be changed by taking this, or any foreseeable, generation of Negroes out of the tropics. As one writer has put it, "the fundamental barrier is less the action of climate on the living generation than its cumulative action, over an immense time-span, in forming the race."

If it be fallacious, why has the doctrine of racial equality become so popular, even among many whites?

A brief glance at history answers this question. The United States was founded primarily by racial stocks which may be loosely defined by the adjective "English-speaking". As Theodore Roosevelt wrote in 1881:

"On the New England Coast the English blood was as pure as in any part of Britain; in New York and New Jersey it was mixed with that of the Dutch settlers—and the Dutch are by race nearer to the true old English of Alfred and Harold than are, for example, the thoroughly Anglicized Welsh of Cornwall. Otherwise, the infusion of new blood into the English race [more accurately, English amalgam] on this side of the Atlantic has been chiefly from three sources—German, Irish, and Norse; and these three sources represent the elemental parts of the composite English stock in about the same proportions in which they were originally combined—mainly Teutonic, largely Celtic, and with a Scandinavian admixture. The descendant of the German becomes as much an Anglo-American as the descendant of the Strathclyde Celt has already become an Anglo-Briton . . . It must always be kept in mind that the Americans and the British are two substantially similar branches of the great English race, which both before and after their separation have assimilated, and made Englishmen of many other peoples. . . . "

This, as I say, was written in 1881. In the later 1880's, conditions began to change. Immigration to the United States shifted from northern to southern and eastern Europe and other branches of the white race, with different temperaments and traditions, arrived in great numbers. The previous record of these stocks for maintaining stable, free societies in their own homelands had not been notably good, although many of them had in other respects backgrounds of the highest culture.

The new arrivals were not readily assimilated. Smarting under what they considered unjustified discrimination, they set purposefully to the task of showing they were just as good as the native stocks (as, indeed, in many ways they were), and they tried to do this by proving that *all* races were equal in their adaptability to our white civilization. Important chairs in several of our leading universities were taken over by these men, and two generations of American youth came under their influence, aided by others whose hearts were softer than their heads were clear. The result was the exploitation of the Boas theories in anthropology, and related doctrines in the field of sociology.

It was only a step to apply these theories to integration. In my opinion, however, they are being applied more to entrench the theories than to help the Negro. Consider the following perhaps unconscious confession on the part of Professor Melville J. Herskovits, an anthropologist who is a member of Boas' own minority group: "Let us suppose it could be shown that the Negro is a man with a past and a reputable past; that in time the concept could be spread that the civilizations of Africa, like those of Europe, have contributed to American culture as we know it today; and that this idea might eventually be taken over into the canons of general thought. Would this not, as a practical measure, tend to undermine the assumptions that bolster racial prejudice?" Professor Herskovits is a man with a self-serving mission. His objectivity as a scientist may be judged accordingly.

There would be something amusing about the works of these men if the gullibility of so many of their readers were not so complete. In addition to their almost incredible prolixity, we find over and over a transparent technique of attempting to destroy truth by ridicule. This technique consists of quoting the older authorities in a context of sneers, with many assertions of their falseness and scientific obsoleteness, and with repeated promises of supporting proof, followed by a change of subject and a failure ever to return to the proof. We might reduce the method to its simplest terms as follows:

"It was the fashion before 1930 to suppose that two plus two equals four. One may be amazed, in the light of modern research, that this belief could have been seriously entertained, but such was the case. Mr. Blank, for example, actually states that two plus two equals four in several of his books, but the dates of these books suffice to discredit him. About 1930, and with increasing frequency ever since, science began to discover that two plus two equals six. Now-a-days, of course, no reputable scientist would suggest anything else. For further discussion of this question, see Chapters 23, 47, and 250."

Upon turning to these chapters we find many wordy paragraphs, but the promised proof recedes before us like a mirage on a desert. The facts are as I have presented them in my letter to the Attorney General and in my answer on pages 44-45. The equalitarians have no defense other than Boas' historical accident and isolation arguments, and these cannot be sustained.

What seems unfortunate is that these white minority groups, to advance what they conceive to be the interests of their special stocks, should promote theories and policies which are bound to weaken the white race as a whole. Like Samson they would pull down the pillars of the temple upon our very heads.

On the other hand, no injustice could be greater than to suppose that all members of the new immigration shared the views, or promoted the policies, of these groups. Many came to America because they understood the native American spirit and desired, not to change it, but to participate in its life. Some of our greatest gains as a nation have come through such individuals.

I will add that membership in a *race* by no means determines membership in a *group*. Among those I hold in bonds of close personal affection I number members of races wholly out of sympathy with the activities in this field of their "minority groups".

The NAACP asserts that there is virtual unanimity among scientists on the biological equality of the Negro. Is this true?

It is not. There is a strong northern clique of equalitarian social anthropologists under the hynopsis of the Boas school which, as I have said in my answer to the preceding question, has captured important chairs in many leading northern and western universities. This clique, aided by equalitarians in government, the press, entertainment, and other fields, has dominated public opinion in these areas and has made it almost impossible for those who disagree with it to hold jobs.

The economic weapon brandished over the head of one's opponent is a common technique of the equalitarian. The non-equalitarian scientists have been forced largely into the universities of the South where they are biding their time. My files provide ample proof of this. One letter from a prominent Northern psychiatrist goes even further, "Where in the U.S. could a psychologist, sociologist or anthropologist find employment if he openly and unreservedly espoused the theory of the racial inequality of man?"[5]

It is folly to talk of freedom, either of the press or of any other kind, when such a situation exists. Probably never in the history of the United States have we seen such a strangle-hold by the national press and other mass media of communication in suppressing the viewpoint of a great section of the country. The extent to which certain of the more authoritative and influential newspapers and magazines, such as the New York *Times* and the *Time-Life* group, are using their columns for sheer propaganda has become laughable. In a moral sense we are confronted with what might almost be called a trilogy of conspiracy, fraud and intimidation: conspiracy to gain control of important citadels of learning and news dissemination, fraud in the teaching of false racial doctrines, and

---

5. A Southern professor of anthropology writes me: "It can be documented *ad infinitum* that the social and biological sciences in Anglo-American countries, for the past half century or so, especially since the twenties, have strenuously and studiously avoided any research that could have thrown light on genetic differences between races and ethnic groups. That this avoidance and suppression, this discouragement of graduate students who might have been curious and interested in such research, was done in the name of the egalitarian ideology, in full knowledge that it was unscholarly conduct, has been admitted, in print, among themselves, by some of our most prominent social scientists."

intimidation in suppressing those who would preach the truth. To speak of academic freedom in the United States today is to make a mockery of the term. This is particularly dangerous in the medical field where suppression of data on sickle-cell anemia and other aspects of Negro biology is common. For those interested in problems of blood transfusion I recommend a reading of "Sensitising Antigens as Factors in Blood Transfusions" by John Scudder, *et al,* in *The Mankind Quarterly* for October 1960. This article has been viciously attacked by equalitarians. I suggest the reader compare the qualifications of the protagonists.

Besides intimidation there has, of course, been a false indoctrination of our younger scientists, although some hope on this score may be found in the following statement in a letter to me from a distinguished scientist younger than I am, a scientist not a Southerner, who is a recognized international authority on the subject we are considering: "About 25 years ago it seemed to be proved beyond a doubt that man is a cultural animal, solely a creature of the environment, and that there is no inheritance of instinct, intelligence or any other capacity. Everything had to be learned and the man or race that had the best opportunity for learning made the best record. The tide is turning. Heredity is coming back, not primarily through anthropologists but through the zoologists. It is the zoologists, the animal behavior men, who are doing it, and the anthropologists are beginning to learn from them. It will take time, but the pendulum will swing."

We may well be amazed, scientists and laymen alike, as we awake from our sleep, at the depth of the hypnosis to which we have been subject. It is true that science has proved that things are not always what they appear, but seldom has a mock science been so successful in making it appear that things are not what they obviously are. I said in my letter to the President that any man with two eyes in his head could make certain observations. How loud does the obvious have to shout before a sensible man will listen?

What I call upon every fair-minded Northerner to do is this: Let him read Boas for himself. Let him read Herskovits and Kluckhohn[6] for himself. These men stand refuted out of their own mouths. I challenge any intelligent person to study their books and come to any other conclusion. I make only one stipulation. Each time the reader finds the phrase: "It has been proved that—" let him ask the question "Where?"

Next, I suggest he talk to some of our non-equalitarian anthropologists who will tell him the truth if he wins their confidence. They will, however, simply be supporting conclusions which he will already have drawn for himself.[7]

Finally, I should point out that anthropologists—apart from their position as equalitarian or non-equalitarian—may be divided into two classes, social and physical. It is the social anthropologists who have led the equalitarian movement although they are the least qualified to pass upon racial biology. The physical anthropologists, along with the physiologists and anatomists, are the ones who are

---

6. In fairness to the memory of the late Clyde Kluckhohn, I should note here that in a review in *The American Anthropologist* in December 1959 (Vol. 61, No. 6) of a book by Walter Goldschmidt, Kluckhohn reversed himself and stated that racial equality in intellect could no longer be assumed. Professor Kluckhohn's words were: "In the light of accumulating information as to significantly varying incidence of mapped genes among different peoples, it seems unwise to assume flatly that 'man's innate capacity does not vary from one population to another' . . . On the premise that specific capacities are influenced by the properties of each gene pool, it seems very likely indeed that populations differ quantitatively in their potentialities for particular kinds of achievement."

7. The layman will find a useful introduction to the anthropological aspects of the integration controversy in Nathaniel Weyl's *The Negro in American Civilization,* (1960), Chapters 11 through 15, together with the footnotes and references contained therein. While I am in sharp disagreement with some of the political and social conclusions which Mr. Weyl projects from his scientific material, the anthropological data are well presented.

To those wishing to go still further into the subject, I recommend, in addition to the works cited by Mr. Weyl, Garrett Hardin's "The Competitive Exclusion Principle," (*Science,* Vol. 131, No. 3409, April 1960); G. Lefrou's *Le Noir D'Afrique* (Payot,106 Boul. St. Germain, Paris, 1943); Georges A. Heuse's *Biologie du Noir* (Les Editions Problemes d'Afrique Centrale, 34 Rue de Stassart, Brussels, 1957); and J. Millot's *Biologie des Races Humaines,* (Librairie Armand Colin, 103 Boul. Saint-Michel, Paris, 1952). The latter books are by European experts of impeccable standing and are considered authoritative by our leading American physical anthropologists. They thoroughly unmask the equalitarian environmentalist doctrine of race. Professor Millot, one of France's two leading anthropologists, warns against racism in the Nazi sense, as well he may, and he makes the same point about the superiority of occasional individuals that I make in answering the question on page 42. He is also at pains to emphasize those faculties of sensory perception, imagination and rhythm in which

expert in this field, but partly because of expense and partly for other reasons, most of our American universities do not have chairs in physical anthropology. Instead, social anthropology has been combined with sociology into one department where each can aid and abet the other in the equalitarian drive.

One's choice of physical anthropologists will therefore be relatively limited in the United States but such men are available upon the terms I mention.

Is Arnold Toynbee a victim of hypnosis?

It depends on how you interpret Toynbee. "It will be seen," he writes, "that when we classify mankind by color, the only one of the primary races, given by this classification, which has not made a creative contribution to any one of our twenty-one civilizations is the Black Race." Then he comments that this "single exception"

---

the Negro surpasses the white man. He makes clear that . . . "The deficiency of the Black appears principally in logical reasoning, in judgment or the capacity to define and analyze with precision, in adaptation to new situations and in the capacity for abstraction. This inferiority seems to result in large part from a precocious arresting of cerebral development."

Dr. Lefrou's book carries an introduction by Professor H. V. Vallois, France's leading anthropologist and head of the Museum of Man. In this introduction Vallois remarks that Lefrou's work "rests on a solid documentation supported by a sure critique," which gives special interest to Lefrou's quotation from Cureau: "There are two quite distinct stages in the intellectual life of the Negro. As a child he is amiable, gentle, gracious, spontaneous and docile. He appears very precocious, more precocious by all odds than the great majority of European children. He understands and easily assimilates many things. At the date of puberty a radical metamorphasis takes place. A sharp arresting of development occurs and even a slight regression. The intellectual progress of the Negro is rapid during the first ten or twelve years, next it slows down, becomes stationary, then proceeds slowly, diminishing during some fifteen years. Finally a rapid enfeeblement occurs."

A caution in regard to Nathaniel Weyl's book is advisable here. It will be noted that on page 246 he belittles the evils of race-mixing, but the cases which he cites are not mixtures of whites and Negroes. On page 244, having suggested that the mulatto is not inferior to the Negro, he uses this as a defense of miscegenation, disregarding its effect upon the white side of the equation. On page 245 he examines and minimizes the effect of the lowering of the I.Q. of the nation as a whole should all Negroes be absorbed, disregarding the fact that the large majority of Negroes are concentrated in the South. It would seem self-evident that Mr. Weyl is reluctant, for certain of the reasons I have already mentioned, to draw the inevitable political conclusions from his own research. His courage in stating the scientific conclusions is commendable.

of the Negro should not prevent the conclusion that "the capacity for civilization . . . is the universal birthright of mankind", and goes on to justify his position by observing that only 6,000 years have elapsed since the first civilizations appeared on earth, and it is perhaps too early to judge whether the Negro is "in a day dream . . . paralyzed . . . or out of the running." Concerning this Toynbee theory, another writer has remarked that "if 60 centuries is too short a period for man to draw general inferences about his past, then Toynbee's life work has been a waste of time."

Toynbee, however, relates his argument to a time-scale which gives it validity in its place. He points out that the Negro still has 83 million times 6,000 years ahead of him, by astronomical calculations, before we can conclude that he lacks the capacity for civilization. On such a time-scale I would agree with Toynbee. In the next 500,000,000,000 years I would be quite prepared to concede the possibility the Negro may, through normal processes of mutation and natural selection within his own race, eventually overtake and even surpass the white race.

The school controversy, on the other hand, is concerned with the present, and with foreseeable future generations. When the Negro has bred out his limitations over hundreds, or thousands, of years, it will be time enough to consider absorbing him in any such massive doses as would be involved in the South today.

Has it not been shown that the skulls of the grandchildren of certain immigrants to the United States are larger than those of their forebears and does this not prove that environment can alter racial capacities?

The skull changes you mention are not sufficient, in either nature or degree, to affect such capacities.

Has not J. C. Carothers suggested that the similarity between the mentality of a European who has had his frontal lobes immobilized by an operation, and the mentality of a normal African may be due to the fact that the African's culture does not place as great a demand on his frontal lobes?

Dr. Carothers suggests this. He also suggests the opposite possibility—that the frontal lobe condition of the African is innate. The truth is that a race must create its culture before the culture can influence the race. It is not a case of the hen and the egg. The race must come first. Or, if one prefers, one may say that a race and its culture in the long run interact upon each other. Whichever way one states it, the fact remains that, if a race has a culture which does not require frontal lobe activity beyond a given threshold, the explanation must lie in the quality of that race's frontal lobes.

Was not Alfred Kroeber a leading anthropologist and does not his "Anthropology" contradict your views?

Alfred Kroeber was indeed a leading anthropologist. As to his contradicting my views, I would say rather that he affords an excellent example of the fact that the older scientists in this field were only partially hypnotized even twelve years ago. At pages 203-204 of the book you mention (ed. 1948), in discussing the question of whether one can rate the hereditary worth of various races according to the number of their men of genius, Kroeber remarks: "A great work naturally requires a great man, but it presupposes also a great culture. It may be that, historically speaking, a great genius cannot arise in a primitive degree of civilization. . . . Biologically the individual of genius may be there; civilizationally he is not called forth. . . . Consequently it is unsound to argue from the historical record to biological worth."

Kroeber here ignores the overwhelming probability that, over the long run, a race capable of producing biological geniuses with sufficient frequency to justify a high rating if they were recognized, would, *in the same long run,* have produced, or caught by contagion,[8] a culture which would have called them forth.

But the example of ambivalence I wish to stress comes in a subsequent paragraph on Kroeber's page 204:

"The drift of this discussion may seem to be an unavowed argu-

---

8. Adherents of the "isolation" defense for the Negro may be interested in Kroeber's comment in a later section of his book: "All in all, Negro Africa lies open enough to the main Eurasian centers to have presumably experienced a slow cultural 'bombardment' that constantly mingled new traits with old, foreign with acclimated, and acclimated elements with those indigenously evolved. Through the centuries and millennia, everything got worked over until it took on the native local color."

ment in favor of race equality. It is not that. As a matter of fact, the anatomical differences between races would appear to render it likely that at least some corresponding congenital differences of psychological quality exist. These differences might not be profound, compared with the sum total of common human faculties, much as the physical variations of mankind fall within the limits of a single species. Yet they would preclude identity. As for the vexed question of superiority, lack of identity would involve at least some degree of greater power in certain respects in some races. These pre-eminences might be rather evenly distributed, so that no one race would notably excel the others in the sum total or average of its capacities; or they might show some minor tendency to cluster on one rather than on another race. In either event, however, race difference, moderate or minimal, qualitative if not quantitative, would remain as something that could perhaps be ultimately determined.

"But it is one thing to admit this theoretical probability and then stop through ignorance of what the differences are, and another to construe the admission as justification of mental attitudes that may be well grounded in historical conditioning but are in considerable measure unfounded objectively."

I offer the above paragraphs as an illustration of the scientific mind in semi-trance, talking out of both sides of its mouth. Or perhaps to the white Southern mother whose child is about to be forced into a predominantly Negro school, it seems more like academic fiddling while Rome burns.

You are preaching a doctrine of white supremacy and allying yourself with lynchers and bombers. Worse, don't you realize that this is the doctrine that led to Hitler's barbaric policies?

I am advocating a doctrine of white leadership based on proved achievement, not supremacy in any sense of domination, exploitation, or violence. As far as the Negro race is concerned, if it is interested in such cultural elements as our white civilization has to offer, it should realize that to destroy or to debilitate the white race would be to kill the goose that lays the golden egg. It is a temptation as old as the human species, and always ends with a dead goose and no eggs.

Regarding Hitler, can we condemn Christianity because of the atrocities of the Spanish Inquisition? Truth has often been warped by evil men to vicious ends. One does not solve the problem by going to the other extreme and embracing error.

In your letter to the President you say the Southern Negro must earn equal status with the white man, yet in your letter to the Attorney General you mention natural limitations which indicate you do not believe the Negro capable of earning it. How do you explain this contradiction?

It isn't really a contradiction. I believe the Negro, if he desires it, should be given every reasonable chance of achieving social and cultural adaptation through equal education in his own schools and by every community effort that does not involve pulling down the white race, but it does not follow that I believe the average Negro capable of achieving it, within any time limits that could have a practical bearing on the present controversy.

Over a matter of hundreds of years, the constant surrounding stimulus of white civilization upon the Negro may be expected slowly to have an adaptive effect. Changes in a race occur by mutation and natural selection which involve the gradual elimination of those genes which are unsuited to the surrounding environment. This takes place by mating choices within the race itself and by the dying-off without children of those with a preponderance of unsuitable genes. The process must obviously be a slow one, involving many generations, before the adapting race can hope to achieve equality. Meanwhile the increasing number of individuals above the average, who are in fact raising the average, should be given every opportunity for the development of their natures within the limits already mentioned.

It is possible, however, to look at the question from a different point of view. Does the Negro really *want* to become like the white man, or will he not in the end prefer to maintain his own racial integrity, eliminating only those factors which conflict with a peaceable life in a predominantly white civilization? In other words, may not the best solution to the problem be permanent voluntary segregation through pride in, and loyalty to, one's own race, Negro as well as white? This would mean adaptation only in those qualities which tend to make the Negro a burden on our white culture and economy, not in others.

This second point of view has been well summarized by the Rev. G. W. Walker, the Negro publisher of the *National Christian Magazine*. The Rev. Mr. Walker says in part:

"We have been given the assignment, the responsibility, the duty, and the obligation:

"1. To teach the Negro the plain and simple view that he has customs, background, consciousness and fundamental characteristics of his own and that he must develop these or else cease to exist as an ethnical identity in America. . . .

"3. To convince the Negro not to desert his own schools, clubs, institutions and churches, but, instead, he must develop them until they are where they should be—on a par with the whites'. . . .

"5. To inform him of the truth, that he has a date with destiny and he cannot keep his date if he integrates and amalgamates with the white race, because this is the sure road or way to a lost race.

"6. To prove to the Negro that integration and race mixing are lethal methods of robbing him of his last chance and only chance to stand on his own two feet and develop a social order of his own, one which he and his true friends can be proud of. . . .

"8. To teach him to stop wanting to be the uninvited guest (rather stranger) in the homes of others and in the places and areas prescribed for others.

"9. To show the Negro that what he really needs for his further advancement and betterment in America is the right kind of education and training, rather than a closer association with white people.

"10. To teach him that aping the white man and trying to be white will dupe him out of his self-respect and the respect of others. . . .

"13. To teach the Negro that there is a vast difference between the white man and himself and that this actual fact must be recognized and dealt with from a realistic and objective point of view.

"14. To teach him that he has many fine qualities, such as kindness, courtesy, loyalty, cheerfulness, gaiety, etc., which are admired and respected by the other races in America and that these fine qualities should be capitalized upon. . . .

"16. To show him his many golden opportunities for greatness in the South, which he is not now utilizing and that he, like the white race, can make great achievements in the South.

"17. To prove to the Negro that it is not morally wrong for his true white friends in the South to wish him to develop his own ways of life, with their friendly help and cooperation; and to teach his own children in his own schools and homes to follow in his own footsteps. . . .

"20. To convince the Negro that it is no disgrace or stigma on his race to be black instead of white and that it is more natural for him to be happier in his own traditions and in his own places than it is for him to be in the traditions and places of the white man. . . .

"28. To convince the Negro that it is not necessary for him to attend integrated schools in the North or in the South, because his true advancement will only come from within his own group. . . .

"38. To teach the Negro to be proud of his own racial heritage and background and to build his future upon the good it has to offer, along with what he has acquired, here in America."

The choice in the long future will be as much the Negro's as the white man's. The Negro may, by cleaving to his own kind, and by adapting to the good rather than to the bad in our white culture, build across the centuries such a race that the white man in the end will be knocking on the Negro's door, rather than vice versa.

Why speak of a character-intelligence index? Does not character follow from intelligence?

Some of the worst criminals in history have been highly intelligent. Conversely, we can all think of friends who are not very keen intellectually, but to whose honor and responsibility we would trust our lives.

Intelligence is almost entirely a matter of heredity. Heredity is also substantially involved in character—ask any man who knows and loves animals—but it is more subject to modification by environment than intelligence.

How can you say singing and athletics do not involve character and intelligence?

I did not say they did not *involve* character and intelligence. I said they were not *primarily* matters of character and intelligence.

Primarily they are physical gifts. While there is no question that every great champion has to have a lion's heart, and other stalwart virtues, these virtues were equally present in cave men. They are desirable in any civilization, but they are not distinctive attributes of an advanced civilization. I might even point out that a canary sings beautifully, and each year a horse wins the Kentucky Derby.

The NAACP maintains that your comparison of the achievements of great white men with those of Negroes is pointless. They say the same comparison could be made between white men and white women, yet no one claims that women are biologically inferior. They also say that the early Irish immigrants to this country were more shabby and lived in poorer shanties than the Negroes. What is your answer?

As to the achievements of women, not even in *Alice in Wonderland* do we find an attempt to equate biological inequivalents. Most women, through history, have been in the home, bearing and rearing children, and to see a Negro man hiding behind a white woman's skirts is just a little sickening.

Concerning the Irish, when the NAACP can point to a Negro city the equal of Dublin or Cork or Belfast, it will be time to discuss it.

Won't human beings gain by the variety and richness of racial mixing? In other words, don't crossings help in breeding?

It depends on what is crossed. Crossing two superior breeds may or may not produce an improvement. Such crossing must be carefully controlled—much more carefully than is possible with human beings—before we can speak with assurance. But one thing is sure: crossing a superior with an inferior breed can only pull the superior down.

American Democracy

Was not American democracy founded on the idea of the equality of all men?

As I have pointed out, Jefferson's phrase, "all men are created equal", which he used in the Declaration of Independence, is a corruption of the original wording as it appeared in the Virginia Declaration of Rights and as it was afterwards copied in many state constitutions. The original wording read: "All men are born equally free," and this was the true foundation of the American ideal. Lincoln, in his Gettysburg Address, simply copied Jefferson's corruption.

It should be noted that Jefferson, in writing the Declaration of Independence, followed the phrase "all men are created equal" with the phrase "they are endowed by their Creator with certain inalienable rights . . . among [which] are life, liberty and the pursuit of happiness." Liberty, in other words, was given the same standing in the Declaration as equality—and a moment's thought will show that the only sense in which equality can co-exist with liberty is in the sense of equality of opportunity. In any other sense, if men are free they won't be equal, and where men are equal they are not free. Hamilton put this point clearly when he said in the Constitutional Convention of 1787: "Inequality will exist as long as liberty exists. It unavoidably results from that very liberty itself."[9]

I would not deny Jefferson's antipathy to slavery, nor the fact that in an early draft of the Declaration he had a reprobation of slavery which he omitted in the final draft because of the opposition of certain signers, nor Lincoln's view that the Declaration was conceived by many as setting up a "standard maxim . . . constantly labored for, and even though never perfectly attained, constantly approximated and thereby constantly . . . augmenting the happiness and value of life to all peoples of all colors everywhere." But as to the majority of signers there can be no doubt of the accuracy of the statement contained in a speech by Stephen A. Douglas in the Lincoln-Douglas debates in 1858:

---

9. For an analysis of the derivation of the "equality" phrase in the Declaration of Independence, see R. Carter Pittman, "Equality Versus Liberty," *American Bar Association Journal,* Vol. 46, No. 8, August 1960.

"Now, I say to you, my fellow-citizens, that in my opinion the signers of the Declaration had no reference to the Negro whatever, when they declared all men to be created equal. They desired to express by that phrase white men, men of European birth and European descent, and had no reference either to the Negro, the savage Indians, the Fiji or the Malay . . . One great evidence that such was their understanding, is to be found in the fact that at that time every one of the thirteen colonies was a slaveholding colony, every signer of the Declaration represented a slaveholding constituency, and we know that no one of them emancipated his slaves, much less offered citizenship to them, when they signed the Declaration; and yet, if they intended to declare that the Negro was the equal of the white man, and entitled by divine right to any equality with him, they were bound, as honest men, that day and hour to have put their Negroes on an equality with themselves. . . .

"My friends, I am in favor of preserving this government as our fathers made it. It does not follow by any means that because the Negro is not your equal or mine, that hence he must necessarily be a slave. On the contrary, it does follow that we ought to extend to the Negro every right, every privilege, every immunity which he is capable of enjoying, consistent with the good of our society."

I call your attention particularly to the last paragraph quoted above, and most especially to the last seven words. On it and them Lincoln and Douglas would certainly have agreed.

It might be noted in passing that the Declaration of Independence is not the charter of our government. The Constitution is the charter, and its preamble states its purpose to be, among other things, to "secure the blessings of liberty to ourselves and our posterity". No mention is made of equality. Of the constitutions and bills of rights of the 48 states as of 1917 (the last available printing) only two use the equality clause of the Declaration of Independence and one of these, North Carolina, had it forced upon her by federal bayonets during Reconstruction. In fact, if one examines the constitutions of all the countries of the world, one finds only four which contain the concept of cultural, economic or social equality. Those four are Guatemala, the Mongol Peoples Republic, the Ukrainian Soviet Socialist Republic and the Union of Soviet Socialist Republics.

Modern equalitarians have not been above practicing certain

deceptions in regard to Jefferson's attitude toward the Negro. On a marble panel in the Jefferson Memorial in Washington is a fragment of one of Jefferson's sentences. As inscribed on the panel the words are: "Nothing is more certainly written in the book of fate than that these people [the Negroes] are to be free." As written by Jefferson, there was no period after these words. There was a semi-colon, and the sentence continued: "Nor is it less certain that the two races, equally free, cannot live under the same government."

Myrdal uses somewhat the same technique in his *Dilemma* when he quotes the first part of Jefferson's sentence at page 85, and postpones any reference to the thought in the second half until five pages later, when he quotes another and weaker sentence from a different volume of Jefferson's writings.

Almost all the great statesmen of our nation's past have foreseen the danger of the Negro among us and have sought to remove it, even to the point of transplanting the race to Africa. The idea of making the Negro the social equal of the white man never entered their heads. Among those beside Jefferson and Lincoln who favored removal to Africa may be mentioned Francis Scott Key, John Randolph, Andrew Jackson, Daniel Webster, and Henry Clay. The modern segregationist is in good company.

Nor should one be beguiled by the equalitarian's claim that this cloud of witnesses is obsolete. The truths involved here are not the sort that become obsolete short of many hundreds, if not thousands, of years.

Does not equality of opportunity for the Negro require desegregation?

If equal facilities, teachers, and curricula are provided, (and where this is not being done, it should be done, and the Supreme Court should have made *this* the issue) there can be no inequality of opportunity. I have already answered, in my letter to the Attorney General, the charge that segregation produces a sense of inferiority, and that a sense of inferiority affects the motivation of a child to learn. What the Negro is really demanding is social equality with a group that does not desire his company. He is in effect saying that unless he has social equality he cannot study as well. A white girl might just as well say that she cannot study unless she is presented at Court.

How can the Negro earn status if he is not given the opportunity to earn it?

This repeats the previous question in a somewhat different form. Segregation, properly administered, as I have said, does not interfere with any Negro getting an equal education if he has the ability and desire. Concerning social status, when, as, and if the average Negro, whether in his segregated school or elsewhere, has on his own initiative evolved into the sort of person with whom the average white man wants to associate, this will soon become apparent to both parties, and segregation will then cease. Social equality cannot be made a condition to the earning of social equality.

It should be kept in mind that every man, black or white, must carry with him to some degree the burden of his background, both as to race and as to family. Let us consider this first from the standpoint of family. To achieve absolute equality at the beginning of every life would require the sacrifice of something even more important, namely, the family, and the responsibility of parents toward their children. One inducement to the good life on the part of a parent is the tradition he passes on. His thrift and self-denial secure his children's education, his character sets an example—to deny a man this influence, for better or for worse, would not only sap the marrow of our civilization, but deny what a majority of Western Europeans would consider a fundamental human right.

The corollary, however, is unavoidable. Not all children have an equal home life in the formative years. The sins and virtues of the father are visited upon his offspring. Both heredity and early environment are unequal. Every white man faces this. Few of us are so fortunate as not to be surpassed in both heredity and environment by someone else, which gives meaning to the old saying: "Life's not in holding a good hand, but in playing a poor one well."

In similar fashion, in the case of race, the sins and virtues of our racial forbears are visited upon their descendants. It might be thought easier, in this instance, to assure each generation a fresh start, but consideration will show that the heritage of race is in part implicit in the family environment and in part in heredity. Both the black and the white child receive a legacy which is a mixture of family and racial heredity and environment. Society can no more make them equal as to the racial component than it can make them equal as to the family component. The problem, according to our Western concept of life, is private because any other theory entails sacrifices greater than the gains.

Isn't it wrong to injure the self-esteem of any man by reflections on his racial background?

No man's self-esteem need be injured by the truth concerning his racial background, any more than an acceptance of innate limitations by people in any sphere need affect their pride. Most of us do not hang our heads in shame if we cannot invent like Edison or write like Shakespeare. As I said in the answer to the preceding question, it is what we do with what we have that counts. We must rouse ourselves to recognize that the equalitarian has no compunction about using the instinct of pity in us to destroy us. It is a classic instance of virtue being kidnapped to serve vice.

Isn't it unfair to discriminate legally against the exceptional Negro on the basis of a racial average?

We discriminate legally against exceptional minors by not allowing them to vote, although certain of them may be more intelligent than many adults. Discriminations of this sort are necessary to the practical administration of human affairs.

Is not the indulgence of personal preference in regard to the company one keeps a right only in private situations? Can one white child avoid another white child whom he considers inferior by insisting he be put in another school?

The question confuses the case of an individual, acting for himself, with the case of the people of a state as a whole, acting by majority rule, or by whatever rule the fundamental law of the state provides. The people thus acting can do anything they please, within certain constitutional limitations. If the majority in a state decide that smokers should be segregated from non-smokers in public conveyances because non-smokers prefer not to associate with smokers in such places, I do not suppose this would be held unconstitutional, although failing such a law, an individual, acting alone, would not have the right to protest. An analagous situation is found in the segregation in separate hospitals of the victims of contagious diseases.

The test is one of reasonableness. The smoker is not harmed, nor the victim of the contagious disease, by segregation with those in a like situation, and if the remainder are benefitted, the public welfare is promoted by the procedure. None of this could be accomplished by a private individual attempting to exercise a personal right to freedom of association.

How can school be considered a "social" situation?

Particularly in rural areas, schools are a social center, but it is true enough elsewhere. There is usually a cafeteria where students lunch together; athletic contests are often held at night and students, following the team, travel in school busses and fraternize before, during and after the game. There are dances. The comments of an 18 year old white girl in an integrated Northern high school published in *U. S. News and World Report,* may properly be quoted here:

"I remember reading somewhere that a famous sociologist said that about the last person that the average white kid would be interested in is a Negro. I have news for him. Integration is a gradual process. At first it is difficult to see anything but that they are Negroes. Later you think of them as just people and then as friends. As one girl I know put it, from there it is just a hop, skip and a jump before you think of them as more than friends. Almost every white girl I knew had a secret crush on one of the colored boys. The crushes varied from warm friendship to wild infatuation ... One of the girls felt guilty about it but she kept on dating the colored boy ... She once told me that if people were going to object they shouldn't expose us to the temptation. As she put it, we're not all saints."

Some integrationists have suggested segregation of the sexes as a solution to this problem but not only would this force the South to give up co-education for white children, it would be at least a poor palliative of the underlying difficulty. As I have said elsewhere, little brother would still bring his new Negro friend home after school. One cannot break down the social barriers among either sex without eventually breaking them down heterosexually.

The technique of gradualism is a notorious one in the progress of equalitarianism, socialism and communism. Seize a little today and it will be easier to seize a little more tomorrow. In fact, all evil, fascist or communist, advances in this manner. One can mention Munich, as well as Moscow. The reason, I think, is that once a principle falls, the inner demoralization has set in, and soon everything else goes. As one respected Southern editor has expressed it in speaking of token integration: "If integration is wrong, as we believe it is, we do not concede that a little bit of it is right." Or, as another well known Southern author has written: "To suppose that we can promote all other degrees of race mixing but stop short of inter-racial mating is like going over Niagra Falls in a barrel in the expectation of stopping three-fourths of the way down."

One other point overlooked by those who dismiss as unimportant the risks of intermarriage in the South is the erosive effect upon personal standards of the equalitarian ideology. This may be expected slowly to overcome many barriers that have hitherto existed. A youth brought up to believe all races potentially equal is first conditioned to disregard the evidence of his senses and the dictates of sound judgment, and then to feel the added pressure of pity. Here, he thinks, is a member of a race which has suffered "cultural deprivation"—not only will time adjust all differences, but marriage may be a recompense for injustice. This dual impact, when added to the factors already mentioned, is well understood by the equalitarian and is counted upon by him to achieve his purpose.

Are not the children themselves perfectly willing to integrate?

A child left to itself is perfectly willing to experiment with anything, including explosives. That is the reason courts appoint guardians for children who have lost their parents.

It must always be remembered that the first thing a group or party that wishes to remake a civilization to suit itself is going to do is to corrupt the relatively defenseless minds of children. The extent to which this process has already succeeded in the North with the generation that has now become adult is alarming enough. Integration is the next step.

If the races, left to themselves, tend to intermarry, doesn't this mean that it is the natural thing to do?

Consider a garden that has been carefully cultivated for many years. What happens if it is left to nature?

Christian Ethics

Does not the Christian religion promise salvation to all men, and are not all men consequently equal in the sight of God?

Yes, as to the first part of this question; no, as to the second. Many people have written me confusing salvation with status. I agree that the Christian religion offers salvation to all true believers, but this has nothing to do with status. Status has to be earned, in religion as elsewhere, by merit. I need only point to Christ's parable of the talents, and of the foolish Virgins, or to the Letter of James, Chapter 2: "You see that a man is justified by works and not by faith alone, for as the body apart from the spirit is dead, so faith apart from works is dead." I may also remind you of the words of Peter, "Make every effort to supplement your faith with virtue, and virtue with knowledge, and knowledge with self-control and self-control with steadfastness and steadfastness with Godliness."

To assume that a person who wastes his life, albeit confident in his redemption through faith, stands on an equal footing before God with a man who strives to progress in character and service, is to make a mockery of the Christian religion. Similarly, to suppose that a good, but weak and stupid man—albeit weak and stupid through environment and heredity rather than through any initial fault of his own—stands other than potentially on the same rank with the good, and strong and intelligent, man within the hierarchy of heaven would be to suppose that God puts no premium on the development of strength and intelligence as either an earthly or heavenly goal. Nothing does greater injustice to the character of Christ Himself. Christ was a Man of infinite compassion, but He was not a Man of maudlin or undiscriminating sentimentality. Christ's life, among other things, might well be called a study in firm discrimination.

But would Christ have discriminated according to race? Was it not always with him a matter of individual worth?

Of course. I have never maintained anything to the contrary. In all matters involving dealings between individuals, where the question of intermarrying is not involved, I think individual worth alone should be the criterion. But there is nothing un-Christian in facing the fact that, as individuals differ in merit, so averages differ among races in those attributes involving specific cultures. Judgments as to the average have to be made accordingly. I must repeat that there are few perfect systems in this world, we have to deal with practical realities, and when we are confronted with a situation where a race must be considered as a race, there is no alternative to building the system around the average. The minor handicap to the exceptional individual, if such there be, is negligible compared to the damage that would otherwise result to society as a whole.

The Christian religion is based upon the concept of growth. We grow as individuals and as races, and not always in the same direction. Individuals or races wishing to move into a society alien to their native culture must have the patience to grow in adaptability and in capacity to contribute to the new culture, and the growth in the case of races takes many generations.

Esme Wynne-Tyson, looking at the subject from the standpoint of England, recently put the matter well in *The Contemporary Review,* one of Britain's leading monthly magazines:

"Almost every man is in a different stage of development, and, even more obviously, are nations and races in different phases of evolution ... It is not a problem that can be solved by any sentimental humanism, or religious insistence that all men are the children of God ...

"The natives of the West Indies have a legal right to enter England as British subjects, but it is not their biological or spiritual home, and may well prevent their natural evolution which can only take place gradually in the environment and culture native to them. On the other hand, the instinctive feeling of many inarticulate but intuitive British people that a mingling of races, which is, more basically, a mingling of two incompatible evolutionary streams, is not 'right,' is a sure one. Specifically they complain of the coloured races being dirty, noisy, or immoral; but these objections are only the outward and visible signs of a different stage of spiritual development, a lower culture, and it is this which is sensed and resented by numbers of British people who have no personal ill-will towards their coloured neighbours as such . . .

"What amounts to an enforced intermingling of white with coloured races in this country at the present time is being resented at a deeper level than most people imagine. The rising generation of British youth is already badly handicapped in its evolutionary struggle by the moral degradation which was involved in, and has resulted from, the last war combined with the wholly unspiritual atmosphere of thought engendered by scientific materialism. And their parents, observing this, cannot submit passively to witnessing their further deterioration through mixing with people of a still lower ethic and culture. The young people of Britain are not themselves sufficiently ethical to instruct their companions how to rise. Evolution is an arduous task. It is far easier to sink than to rise.

"We have an object lesson of this in modern America which has badly suffered from close propinquity with its less evolved immigrants. The 'hot' music, primitive dances, and other sensual practices of the coloured races, have permeated with their devolutionary influences, every corner of a once-Puritan civilization, debasing and obstructing the process of an originally highly ethical people. Hence the instinctive fear lying at the back of much of the present colour prejudice in this country [England]."

It may be too late to return the American Negro to his biological and spiritual home, but it may not be too late to redeem in America the heritage of the white race. Unless this is done, it will not be long before many a white man in the United States will have cause to paraphrase De la Mare's lines:

"This is not the place for me;
Never doubt it, I have come
By some dark catastrophe
Far, far from home."

What's the use in trying to convince my mind when my heart tells me segregation is wrong?

In the twenty-second chapter of St. Matthew's gospel, you will find these lines: "Then one of them, which was a lawyer, asked him a question, tempting him and saying, Master, which is the great commandment in the law? Jesus said unto him, Thou shalt love the Lord thy God with all thy heart, and with all thy soul, and with all thy mind. This is the first and great commandment."

There seems little doubt that most of our difficulties are due to a failure to use our minds as well as our hearts, and that more of the evil in the world is created by fools than by knaves. Well intentioned, but ignorant or stupid, people are at the bottom of most of the world's troubles. The heart, unguided by wisdom, soon leads us into emotionalism and thence into chaos. I have often recalled Dickens' reference to the "first mistaken wanderings of an undisciplined heart" in watching some of the tragedies of youth, and I have seen much the same process in adults. Unless the heart and the mind work together, there is no hope for success in the pursuit of happiness by the individual or society. In a prayer I once heard, the pastor used a phrase which I recommend to you, "Lord, help our hearts to think straight."

Why do many leaders of the modern church support the integration movement?

Because they have accepted uncritically the anthropological doctrines of the Boas clique. They have forgotten the commandment to worship God with all their minds as well as with all their hearts.

Don't you believe in the brotherhood of man?

Yes, when this concept is correctly understood. I believe that just as charity begins at home (although it should not end there), so brotherhood begins with the family. The communist technique of undermining the family as a social unit is very much of a part with their pressures for racial integration. The communists wish to kill any loyalties other than to "the State". But the Christian social structure, like many others, is built upon the unit of the family. It recognizes the natural impulse of men to group themselves around their own kind. Birds of a feather flock together. This does not prohibit cooperation and sympathy beyond the family—in the community, the state, and throughout the world. However, the process, to be sound, must source in the primary natural unit of the home, and the "brotherhood of man" must be understood in this light.

The important thing is to recognize that the grouping instinct is basic, and that race is one of the wider groups. To preach against its manifestations is not only a perversion of ideals, but a very effective way of destroying a civilization.

Why worry so much about the future? Why not adopt the policy that will help the Negro most today, if it doesn't hurt the present generation of whites?

Wynne-Tyson has pointed out (page 69) that our contemporary American civilization is suffering already from the deteriorating effects of too indiscriminate an acceptance of various features of other cultures.

Deterioration of this sort spreads rapidly. "It is far easier to sink than to rise." To expose young white children, in their most formative years, to the Negro influence would have an immediate adverse effect.

Sociology And Communism

Is not the segregationist's position dated from the standpoint of modern sociology?

Modern sociology is too often found to be the child of modern equalitarian anthropology. But let me make clear my position on the broader sociological question, as distinguished from my position on integration, the latter being only a facet of the former.

I believe the real contest in America today is between equalitarianism on the one hand, and individual freedom and responsibility on the other. One of the notions inherent in the first system is the idea that benefits should flow from the State; in the second, that benefits should flow from individual effort. Although I doubt if they realize it themselves, modern writers on social questions are betrayed by the fact that their works almost never contain the words "earn" or "deserve." It never seems to occur to them that one man might be rich because he deserved to be, while another might be poor for the same reason — indeed, that in America this is far more often the case than otherwise, and that one does not cure improvidence and bad self-management by rewarding it at the expense of thrift and foresight.

The trend is particularly damaging in the training of the young. Let us not forget that civilized living, thoughtfulness of others, honesty, thrift, sexual loyalty, have to be taught, even though the capacity to absorb the teaching varies. And let us not forget that you cannot teach the value of something unless you devalue its opposite, that you cannot create superior ideals and superior people by pretending that inferior ideals and inferior people—black or white —are just as good.

While I think that our society has been correct in putting a floor under failure, in relieving undeserved misery, and in curbing business buccaneering, I believe it has been wrong in allowing the whole emphasis to be shifted from self-dependence to State dependence. The application of my point to the integration controversy can be expressed in the words of one of my correspondents:

"In the last ten years, or ever since the decision was made by the leftwingers to enlist the Negro in their crusade for universal erosion, the leadership of the Negro race has almost abandoned efforts at self-improvement by the Negro. In my lifetime the patient pioneering of Southern leaders, both white and Negro, had, I believe, led to some improvement, both in race relations and in the status of the Negro in the American communities.

"Now virtually all the emphasis is being placed upon the theory that the big obstacle to a millenium for the Negro race is the oppressive social system under which he lives. Even a far more sophisticated and superior race of people would be corrupted by such a narcotic as this. In the case of the Negro, with his uncritical mind and lack of experience, the result has been nothing less than a catastrophe."

Are not adverse circumstances the cause of most failures, and is not most of the evil in the world the fault of defective human institutions?

Here is another equalitarian tenet that has spread through our society like a cancer. Myrdal begins one of his chapters with this sentence: "The liberal is inclined to believe that it is the occasion that makes the thief, while the conservative is likely to hold that the thief is likely to create the occasion." It would be hard to find a more obvious effort to win sympathy for the equalitarian viewpoint through a fallacious generality.

The accurate way of stating the case is: "The equalitarian believes that the occasion makes the thief; the genuine American liberal holds that occasions may indeed be bad enough to make a thief of any man, and that society should strive to alleviate such conditions and succor their victims, but that on the average, in the long run, a man is himself responsible for his circumstances." The only qualifications I would place on this re-statement are contained in my answer to the question beginning on page 63.

Just as no victory can compare with the victory of a man over himself, so no defeat can be greater than that which comes to the individual and to society when men are taught to blame their failings on anything and anybody but themselves. Evil as other conditions may be, this is the greatest of all evils, because it destroys the core of human character.

Is it true that integration is part of the communist conspiracy in America?

The communists have made the integration movement a part of their conspiracy, although of course communism is not the only force back of integration. Communism is one phase of a disease, of which equalitarianism and socialism are milder phases, all of which stem from the general leftist overdrift.

However, I believe the equalitarian ideology, which presumes to justify integration, is playing into communist hands, not only by setting section against section in America, but by spreading the equalitarian virus, and thus weakening the body politic to a point where more dangerous phases of the disease are contracted. Khrushchev tells every American he meets that the latter's grandchildren will be living under socialism. Khrushchev cares little by what name his rose is called, but we are beginning to feel its thorns.

Obviously, "the State" is a purely theoretical concept which exists only in the mind. The sole flesh-and-blood, material reality is the individual. "The State" is no more than a name which individuals give to a method they use for working together to achieve certain objects these individuals desire. Therefore, when any individual or group of individuals talks of dependence on the State, they are talking of some individuals depending on other individuals, a procedure which in the end either makes the individuals who are depended on rebel, or makes them use the dependence to exploit the parasites by way of compensation.

Communism, of course, carries this exploitation to the limit. In the process, and to confuse the minds of the exploited, it seeks to warp the flesh-and-blood reality of the individual into its exact opposite. In a tract used in a communist school for subversives in Milwaukee I find the following paragraph:

"Man is already a colonial aggregation of cells, and to consider him an individual would be an error. Colonies of cells have gathered together as one organ or another of the body, and then these organs have, themselves, gathered together to form the whole. Thus we see that man, himself, is already a political organism, even if we do not consider a mass of men."

It seems strange that anyone could be blind enough not to realize at once that the only *entity of consciousness* in the situation is the person—that neither the cell nor the State can ever qualify in this respect—but these are the sort of stupidities one must expect as the disease of equalitarianism progresses.

The sad thing is that the Santa Claus aspect of equalitarianism—the idea that "the State" is a mystic something that can be leaned on—is very beguiling to ignorant and backward peoples. The easy handout, the Santa Claus image, does indeed become a narcotic. It not only drugs groups of individuals within the nation, but it operates between nations. Probably there has never been as soft a touch internationally as Uncle Sam today in the minds of backward peoples. I do not say that the image is correct, but I say that it is there, and that if we encourage it, it can become real and thus destroy us. For we are not ruthless enough to exploit, and it may be too late to rebel.

Does not the support of integration by our wealthy foundations suggest that they have been taken over by communism?

Certainly not consciously. But I think there is a tendency upon the part of men managing large sums of private capital to defend themselves against attacks as capitalists by over-proving themselves in the opposite direction. The same has been true, and still is true, of wealthy men in politics. This again plays into communist hands.

One episode which I must say startles me is the Carnegie Foundation subsidy of Myrdal's *American Dilemma.* There is much interesting material in this book, but the approach is wholly equalitarian. I could not help thinking of the Carnegie Foundation when I read the following passage from a speech of welcome which Beria made to American student subversives at a class on Psychopolitics at Lenin University:

"To produce a maximum of chaos in the culture of the enemy is our first most important step ... You must work until every teacher of psychology unknowingly teaches only Communist doctrine under the guise of 'psychology'. You must labor until every doctor and psychiatrist is either a psycho-politician or an un-witting assistant to our aims . . . Use the courts, use the Constitution of the country, use its medical societies and its laws to further our ends. Do not stint in your labor in this direction. And when you have succeeded you will discover that you can now effect your own legislation at will and you can, by careful organization of healing societies, by constant campaign about the terrors of society, by pretense as to your effectiveness, make your Capitalist himself finance a large portion of the quiet Communist conquest of the nation."

Does not our democracy need to practice equalitarianism at home in order to fight communism abroad?

You do not fight a disease by contracting it. Or, to put the matter another way, if a gangster offers your child opium to get him to join his side, you do not also offer him opium to keep him on yours. Moreover, competent observers, both in our foreign service and in business, who have returned from backward countries, have repeatedly told me that one reason Americans are so often held in secret, if not open, contempt in those countries is that Americans are willing to give with no conditions, are timid about exacting anything in return, and make no demand that the help granted be as far as possible earned and deserved. Raise a child in that way and you have a delinquent. There is no more fundamental truth in life than that status to be worth anything has to be earned, whether by races or by individuals. There is something in the most primitive man that recognizes this truth, and respects and tries to emulate the person or race that asserts it.

Consider in this connection the following remarks by Albert Schweitzer, probably the world's greatest practicing humanitarian and a specialist on the African Negro. No equalitarian can be compared with Schweitzer when it comes to giving his life to help the black man. The quotation is from Schweitzer's book *On the Edge of the Primeval Forest:*

"The Negro is a child, and with children nothing can be done without the use of authority. We must, therefore, so arrange the circumstances of daily life that my natural authority can find expression. With regard to the Negroes, then, I have coined the formula: 'I am your brother, it is true, but your elder brother'.

"The combination of friendliness with authority is the great secret of successful intercourse. One of our missionaries, Mr. Robert, left the staff some years ago to live among the Negroes as their brother absolutely. He built himself a small house near a village between Lambaréné and N'Gomo, and wished to be recognized as a member of the village. From that day his life became a misery. With his abandonment of the social interval between white and black he lost all his influence."

The white man who preaches to backward races a doctrine of equality not only demeans himself and his own race, but forfeits his opportunity to be of real service. What is called the "liberal ferment" among backward peoples who are shouting democracy from Latin America to Africa is too often not at all a struggle for freedom under law on the part of peoples capable of self-government, as was the case in the American Revolution, but rather a demand for license under lawlessness on the part of peoples totally incapable of self-government. As the aforesaid foreign observers have so often reported, and as any traveler can confirm for himself, these peoples do not really desire or understand freedom and its responsibilities; they wish equality and the capture for themselves of the fruits of the intelligence and enterprise of others. They wish white men to continue pumping in capital and management while they take over the product. For evil or stupid whites to encourage ferment of this sort is folly and retrogression for all concerned. Before we press too hard for the handing over of all colonial empires to the natives, we had better ask ourselves whether we are ready to give the United States back to the Indians and whether humanity as a whole would be better off if we did.

There is a noticeable similarity between many of the hat-in-hand arguments of the racial and backward-country pressure groups and the typical panhandler on the street. There is always the hard-luck story, and on investigation there is usually found to be the same reason back of the hard luck. If you keep on giving the dimes or the dollars without insisting on the panhandler at the same time doing something for and about himself, there is no progress, and eventually you, also, are penniless.

Let us consider another aspect of the matter. In many instances, when the white colonial powers moved into the more backward areas, they put a stop to all sorts of horror and cruelty. Liberals and churchmen cried out to have this done, just as they now cry out to turn the natives back to the freedom that originally produced the horror. Writing in 1893 of conditions in Kenya, where Tom Mboya now vies for power with Jomo Kenyatta, the "bloody spear" of the Mau Mau, Lord Lugard said:

" . . . Such is African life, for the African knows no peace.

"One day you may see peace and plenty, well-tilled fields and children playing in the sun; on the next you may find the corpses of the men, the bodies of the children half-burnt in the flames which consumed the village, while the women are the captives of the victorious raiders. Not against the slave trade alone are our efforts needed. The Pax Britannica which shall stop this lawless raiding and this constant intertribal warfare will be the greatest blessing Africa has known through the ages since the Flood."

We have no assurance whatever that granting "freedom" in these areas will not simply restore the old miseries and barbarity whose very existence Christian nations found unbearable. Are such nations going to stand aside while practices such as those mentioned on page 44 are resumed?

It does not solve the problem to talk about "winds of change" sweeping continents, or to take the attitude that we are forced by inevitable trends to adopt equalitarian policies. This is the very notion by which the equalitarian hypnotizes us. Let us realize the truth: It is the false ideology which has produced the change, not the change which requires the false ideology.

American economic aid saved Europe. Might not a similar plan help the backward peoples of the world?

Here we face another danger of our uncritical acceptance of the doctrine of equal racial capacities.

The peoples of Europe long ago proved their capacity for industrial civilization and, in many cases, for freedom. To put them back on their feet was one thing. To put races on their feet who have never been there, either industrially or as free societies, is a different matter.

It may be possible to do this over a long period of time and with firm discipline, but we had better be sure we do not destroy ourselves in the process. Just as everybody is against sin, so everyone is against poverty and human misery. The question which the man who earns the money, as distinguished from the spender, has to ask is, how much more can I stand? Every practical philanthropist knows that it does the community no good to save your neighbor if you then take his place in destitution.

It is also well known that once you whet the appetite of certain groups for spending the money of other groups—and this applies to the international as well as the national community—it becomes almost insatiable. It demands more and more, and will not tolerate weaning. As a noted Democrat expressed it in the days before the New Deal: "Once the doors of a government treasury are thrown open, they are seldom closed except with gunpowder."

Another side of the subject which has been completely misrepresented by the equalitarians is the idea that free societies, which they love to call "democracies" because the word has a certain connotation of equality which "freedom" and "republic" do not have, can be established and maintained by a snap of the fingers. This offers, from their point of view, the additional advantage of devaluing the achievement of those peoples who through long centuries of travail finally produced the great free societies of the Western world.

As I have already indicated, a stable, free civilization is first a matter of individual character in a population. Individual frugality leads to balanced public budgets, individual self-control leads to public law and order and to that absence of emotionalism so necessary to the rule of reason in parliamentary assemblies and in jury trials, individual self-reliance lightens the weight of taxation, and individual forethought leaves no man with the feeling that from the harvest of his effort he is paying for the shiftlessness of someone else. These are the qualities on which a free society rests. How many of them exist among backward peoples, especially among those with heavy admixtures of Negro genes?

In a recent speech at the University of Virginia, Adlai Stevenson remarked that the American Revolution "belonged to the world." I would like to ask Mr. Stevenson by what process of reasoning he compares the capacity for self-government of the American colonists of 1776—inheritors as Englishmen of half a millennium of experience since Magna Carta both in earning and in managing an increasingly free society—with the capacity of the backward peoples of the world today.

Stevenson's remark strikes me as a new low in international demagoguery, but at the same time it is typical of the glib, high-sounding nonsense of many of our equalitarian "leaders." It is quite as feasible to give the American tennis championship to Eleanor Roosevelt as to give the American Revolution to the backward peoples of the world.

I do not wish to suggest that Americans should turn a deaf ear to the aspirations of any people who may be helped to help themselves. That kind of leadership is both our privilege and our duty as a Christian nation. My criticism is of the absurd time schedule, and other methods of procedure proposed by the equalitarians. Consider the Philippines. Here the United States was dealing with a race far higher in adaptability to Western civilization than the Negro, yet it took forty years of careful preparation before the Philippines were thought ready for independence. They still have numerous growing pains. By what possible process of rationalization can we assume the African Negro, among the lowest on the scale of races, can be granted freedom on the spur of a moment? The problem is one not of years or decades but of centuries before any self-sustaining democracies worthy of the name can be developed.

Finally I would point out the folly of granting "independence" to areas where the native populations are totally incapable of maintaining even a modicum of law and order, or of protecting investments or human life. Such a policy creates a power vacuum into which the Russians move at once. The end result can only be an exchange of masters, a jumping from the frying pan into the fire, plus a loss to the free world of the chance to develop the areas in question either politically or economically. The best hope now would seem to lie in the United Nations, if such a body proves equal to the arduous police and other responsibilities required. We cannot talk in one breath, as even Eisenhower is wont to do, of giving a "nation" of savages complete internal "freedom" and then talk, in the next breath, of supplying that "nation" with investments and civilized aid. Investments, and the civilized people administering them, need protection. They cannot be poured into a bottomless pit of chaos.

However, the point to note is the blindness of not realizing in the first place that this protection would be necessary, a blindness characteristic of the victims of equalitarian propaganda. Note also the tragedy and danger in arousing among the natives expectations that cannot be fulfilled.

Are not the new African nations justified in hating colonialism?

The colonial powers have differed in their attitudes towards the natives, some having been more progressive than others, but none has failed to improve the condition of these natives by comparison with their condition in the savage state.

It is certainly unreasonable to expect the attitude of a colonial power to be based solely on philanthropy. Fairness requires some compensation for effort and capital invested. Only missionaries can be expected to be entirely free of self-interest, and missionaries were as ruthlessly raped and murdered in the Congo as other whites.

As elsewhere, so here, the equalitarian tries to teach us to give something for nothing, and to do so at an ever-accelerating rate. The Black, moreover, is canny, and will play white men against each other on the international stage just as he is playing them against each other in our domestic politics. Let us not suppose for a moment that the average African Negro is about to understand our ideals, or to fight or sacrifice or die for the principle of liberty. All he wants, as I have said, is a greater and greater share of what white men have created, regardless of his ability either to protect, manage or pay for it. And if allowed to do so, he will side with whoever seems likely to give him the most, not of freedom, whose responsibilities he cannot assume, but of material gifts. [10]

---

10. Stuart Cloete, the noted writer on African affairs, has this to say about conditions in the Congo: "I have yet to meet more than a handful of Africans who wanted to work. There are a few, but so few that they can be considered non-existent . . . There is no desire to succeed here—only an unearned claim for equality with nations

I am led to stress again here the debasing business practiced by our political leaders when they talk of bribing Africans at the expense of white children in the South. "We must integrate," they say, "to win the favor of these Africans and prove to them we believe in the democratic ideals we profess." I have already considered the absurdity of this position as far as it concerns American democracy. The more disgusting aspect of the matter is the currying of favor, the fawning, and finally the human sacrifice offered them on the altar of this absurdity. Let me repeat what I said on page 75: You do not lift the inferior up by pulling the superior down. You do not elevate savages by lowering your own standards—they gain nothing but glut, and you lose the last shred both of their respect and of your own self-respect. The performance of our "leaders" on this score is perhaps the most revolting in the entire integration controversy.

Since the world is two-thirds colored, and the white race is thus badly outnumbered, are not whites foolish to antagonize the rest of humanity by claiming superiority?

The world is not two-thirds Negro. We are not concerned here in any way whatever with the yellow race, for example, which has proved itself capable of the most advanced forms of self-sustained culture.

But even if the world were nine-tenths Negro, I would still point out to you that leadership is always confined to a numerical minority. If this leadership renounces its confidence in itself, and its authority, because it is outnumbered, whence shall progress come?

---

that have spent millennia climbing out of barbarism. The African is still in an infantile stage of violence. He cannot think, argue or rationalize. His answer to any problem is the spear, the club or the witch doctor . . . Like a delinquent, the Congo out of control will have to be institutionalized . . . It is we who are going to foot the bill for rehabilitation. The flood of dollars has already begun. It will be interesting to see into whose pockets it flows since most of the money spent by the United Nations will come from us. It is we who will pay the piper and yet not call the tune."

In regard to other Negro states, Mr. Cloete writes: "Without white direction and control he [the Negro] can do nothing. There are no African achievements. Ghana is believed to be running on an even keel, but if the white man left Ghana it, too, would collapse. Liberia is supported by Firestone and the Bona Hills iron mines. Haiti is always in distress; Abyssinia, dependent on white enterprise."

Is not white arrogance the cause of most of the resentment among backward peoples?

It depends on what is meant by "arrogance". If by it is implied a domineering, hostile attitude, I would say this might well cause resentment anywhere. But if you mean a maintaining of Schweitzer's "social interval"—the "I am your brother, it is true, but your elder brother" attitude—then I would say the resentment is unjustified.

Perhaps I should add that I have noticed a tendency for indignation long frustrated to become arrogance of the former sort in all but the most charitable natures.

Isn't your philosophy authoritarian?

As I understand it, the word authoritarian applies to one who favors the substitution of authority for individual liberty as a political ideal among peoples capable of self-government. Nothing I have said suggests such an inclination on my part. But I cannot protest too strongly against the tendency of the equalitarian virus to undermine all authority in our society from the home through the school on into our attitude toward international affairs. I suppose it follows from an ideology which assumes the equality of all men that no man is worth listening to more than another, no idea is more valuable than another, no child wiser than its parents, no code higher or more authoritative than another.

But it happens that in the course of human history much has occurred and much has been learned which constitutes a fund of experience we disregard at our peril. All of us are *not* as wise as our ancestors. We can become wiser only by listening to their experience before going on to add our own, just as a child must first listen to his parents before he can safely lead a life of his own.

What is more serious, the destruction by the equalitarian virus of this proper and necessary kind of authority also destroys proper and necessary discipline. Lack of it in the home is, in my opinion, far more often the cause of juvenile delinquency among both rich and poor than the so-called exclusion from family or community groups which today obsesses psychiatrists and sociologists. Perhaps an ideology which offers ice cream to soothe mutinous convicts, and which condones murder and robbery among backward peoples under the guise of "freedom", should not be expected to create respect for duly constituted authority in the home. Yet all children, and especially delinquents, need to be taught respect for and obedience to parental authority if we are ever to have law and order in the adult world.

Interestingly enough, the delinquent who is capable of being saved wants the voice of authority to rebuke and guide him more than he wants pity and tears. Parents are usually to blame both in failing to set an example that can be respected and in failing to speak with the tone of command. Men or nations that have been told often enough that in spite of all their training, experience and wisdom they are no better than the untrained, inexperienced and ignorant child or race will come in time to believe it, and consequently to lose the force and assurance which generates obedience.

Finally, by a series of insidious steps the equalitarian virus produces that most disastrous of all diseases, the complete appeasement of evil. At some point, all ability to discriminate is lost, all resistance to wrong ceases, all indignation dies, all evil is met with sobbing pleas which evil most naturally greets with contemptuous laughter, and the red death of a Godless communism settles on the earth.

Let those of us who are Christians remember that while Jesus could weep, he also could take a lash to the desecrators of the temple.

Aren't you an extreme rightist?

Not in the sense that you are probably using the word. We are too apt to catalogue people into right or left instead of into right or wrong.

As I have already said, I am fully aware of the dangers of unregulated freedom to harm others. When freedom becomes license it has to be curbed. Freedom to murder cannot be tolerated at the individual level, and there are analagous freedoms which have to be curbed on the social level.

Usually the term "rightist" is used by leftists to suggest a man who favors unlimited license to plunder others on the social level, through business monoplies, sweat shops, colonial exploitation, union busting and the like. But the true conservative realizes that every healthy society has to regulate its freedom. The point is that such regulation does not justify leaping into equalitarianism. All health is a matter of balance, just as the smooth running of an automobile is a matter of the proper mixture. My position is that both domestically and internationally our social carburetor has been put dangerously out of adjustment to the left. The engine is beginning to miss. Unless the mixture is corrected, the engine will stop as surely as if the adjustment were too far to the right.

You must be a very old man living in the past. Have you no liberal views?

Your question reminds me of the story of the envoy from the French Government to the court of Queen Victoria who found that the Queen was annoyed because in his youth he had fought on the barricades in the revolution of 1830. When she taxed him with this, he replied: "Your Majesty, not to be a socialist at twenty denotes a want of heart; to be a socialist at forty denotes a want of head."

I will admit that I am over forty, but perhaps I should add that I am still on the sunny side of sixty. I have many liberal views. Let me refer you to what I said in my answers on pages 72 and 83.

Why do the leaders of both our major political parties close their eyes to the Southern viewpoint?

Partly through ignorance of its scientific validity. But this ignorance they are inclined to cherish, and to avoid correcting, because of the balance of power held by Negro voters in certain key states. The situation has been well presented by James Reston of the New York *Times* who points out that in 1948 President Truman carried Illinois by 33,612 votes with the Negro vote for him in Chicago alone being about 90,000. In the same election, the Democratic majority in California was 17,865 and in Ohio 7,107. In both of these states, as in Illinois, the Negroes gave the Democratic party far more than the number of votes needed to win.

The tragedy is that the great majority of Americans are dividing their votes on *other issues* in such a way as to give *this issue* into the hands of the minority. The Republican party pays lip service to Lincoln yet continues to advocate policies to which Lincoln was, and would be today, violently opposed. The Democratic party glorifies Jefferson yet would force on the South conditions which would make Jefferson turn in his grave. Could the race question be isolated so that it could first be thoroughly debated and then voted on by itself alone, the minority would be swamped.

Is not the South backward in every respect and is not its attitude toward the Negro typical?

The agricultural economy of the South was ruthlessly destroyed by the Civil War and Reconstruction. There was no Marshall Plan to help the South, and many years have been required to rise from the poverty that ensued and to begin the industrialization that is now well under way. The North did its best to break the South materially and spiritually a hundred years ago, and it ill behooves Northerners to criticize the results now.

Least of all can the North afford to condemn the South for backwardness in matters involving its cultural heritage, since in this respect the South has done far better than the North. I draw your attention to the fact that what I have called the "new immigration" has concentrated very largely in the urban northeast and north-central sections of the United States, has bred prolifically there, not only in children but in ideas, has come to wield a heavy influence in the educational and entertainment fields and in other areas of mass communications, and finally that this "new immigration" was not initially schooled in the Protestant Ethic[11] upon which our nation was founded. Nor has it shown any great inclination to become so.[12]

---

11. This term is subject to many interpretations. I use it in the broadest sense of that morality and those principles which are based upon the Christian religion as it has been interpreted by the vast majority of the English-speaking peoples. Individualism, thrift, earning and deserving—these are a few of the concepts I would include under the term, but these are not to be extended to cover their caricatures in greed, parsimony and selfishness.

12. For a provocative study of the effect of cultural mixing throughout history, and the initial deterioration that can be expected from it, see J. M. Radzinski "The American Melting Pot: Its Meaning to Us," *American Journal of Psychiatry*, Vol. 115, No. 10, April 1959. Dr. Radzinski says in part: "The immigration of many millions of people into the U.S.A., *particularly during the past 80 years,* [Emphasis mine: this was the period of immigration of non-English speaking peoples in the sense this term is used in my answer on page 47] has brought together here the greatest assortment of ethnic stocks in the world and probably in history. If the lessons of European experience have any meaning, such a conglomeration of racial and ethnic elements renders a serious cultural decline inevitable. Symptoms of the decline are already apparent in the deteriorating state of some aspects of our culture, in the irresoluteness and confusion of our national leaders and in the virulence of frank antisocial behavior among our people far in excess of that encountered in west European countries, Canada and Australia . . . Today, in excessive homicide, treason, juvenile delinquency and other crimes with their tremendous cost in suffering and treasure, we are paying the price for our reckless generosity to peoples of other lands."

In the South, on the other hand, we have a purer concentration of those stocks which were schooled in the Protestant Ethic than anywhere in the urban North. I recognize that the West has produced its native left-wing movements out of stocks largely Protestant in culture, and that England itself has gone further in its socialistic experiments than we have, but in those phases of cultural deterioration which involve an attack upon the Protestant Ethic in its moral aspects our urban North easily leads.

Does not each new generation always disagree with the older generation and is this not a part of progress?

Sometimes the disagreement means progress, sometimes not. A friend of mine in New England recently remarked that she found practically no one under fifty willing even to listen to any point of view other than the equalitarian, whether in matters of race or in other fields. She spoke of it as a closed-mindedness she found hard to understand, and she was aghast at being called intolerant when the intolerance was so obviously on the other side.

I told her I thought the trouble originated in something more profound, that it ended in closed-mindedness but that it started with the hypnosis I mention in my answer beginning on page 50. Her choice of the age of fifty is interesting. If the average person who goes to college finishes at twenty-two, the people who are fifty today were graduating in 1932 at the depth of the depression. Everyone younger received his education under the New Deal when the equalitarian hypnosis was deepening steadily. These figures approximately coincide with the anthropological trance of 25 years ago mentioned by the scientist I quote on page 50.

The young minds formed in the North[13] in the mid-thirties and later are indeed closed, and the trance closing them is one of the most serious problems in the free world. The unreality, the fraudulent assumptions, dinned into them in those days now simply re-echo to us from what seem to be adult minds. This situation has produced a condition quite different from the normal disagreement between younger and older generations.

---

13. Somewhat the same situation occurred in the South, although to a lesser degree because in the South discerning youth had always before it the reality of the Negro.

Normal progress would have involved a continuation of the social justice programs begun under the first Roosevelt and Woodrow Wilson. For example, the *earn-deserve* concept so vital to a healthy society would have been retained along with the objective of helping others to help themselves. This concept and this objective would have been carried forward into areas where social injustice still existed.

It has never been my contention that we should go back to a *laissez-faire* society. I hold no brief for twelve-hour days or child labor. I am perfectly aware that the end of free land, the increase in our population and the advance in industry and science made obsolete many doctrines of the McKinley era. Where I call a halt is the point at which the Marxist jumps on the liberal bandwagon, grabs the reins and drives it down the blind alley of equalitarianism.

Helping people to help themselves, spending money in the public domain for the benefit of all the people, and taxing ourselves for that purpose is one thing. Preaching a thinly veiled Robin Hood philosophy of government, buying the votes of the more numerous with promises to rob the less numerous, taxing the provident to sustain the improvident, and above all forcing cultural deterioration upon fifty million people in the South on false doctrines of racial equality is something else.

It seems to me that the distinction I draw here is the decisive one between the true liberal and the equalitarian. The liberal desires to improve the condition of mankind by creating an inspirational climate. He knows that life's challenges make its inequalities, and vice versa. He knows that you cannot have excellence unless someone excels. He knows that human souls, like human muscles, grow through effort—spiritual, moral and intellectual effort. The equalitarian knows these things, too, but he wants neither challenges nor excellence. He envies the excellence he either cannot achieve, or will not pay the price of achieving. And so he does what he can to destroy inducements to excellence. He fans the envy of others. He persuades them that excellence is injustice to themselves. He works to create a spiritual, moral and intellectual climate favorable to mediocrity. He levels down, and he uses the instinct of pity in good-natured people as part of his technique.

It is, perhaps, in the area of race that the equalitarian most openly betrays himself. Even those in the deepest trance are dimly aware of the falseness of their position, its obvious evils at home and abroad, yet the total hypnosis is so strong that they can only blunder on, rationalizing and evading the endless contradictions in which they find themselves. Over and over they call themselves "liberals" and their cause the cause of "human rights" forgetting that instead of granting human rights to Negroes they are stealing them from whites and are accessories before the fact in the rape of a civilization.

Is not the NAACP doing a great work for the Negro?

An Association for the Advancement of Colored People *could* do a great work for the Negro. But I believe that the emphasis of the present Association is wrong for the reasons given in the quotation on page 72. Undoutbedly, education in many Negro schools can be improved. Undoubtedly, economic opportunities for Negroes can be increased and cultural opportunities for them expanded. Most of all, solutions to their crime rate, irresponsibility, moral delinquency and other limitations can be sought. These are the areas in which the Negro can be helped. In the long run, it does him only harm to encourage him to blame others for his own shortcomings. It is particularly harmful to encourage ingratitude, insolence and aggressive imposition on the whites of the South.

Under equalitarian influence, with a strong assist from communism, it has become the fashion in the North to regard the Southern Negro as the victim of oppression, while the truth is that the Negro in the South is on the whole the product of a friendliness and helpfulness unequalled in any comparable instance in all history. As one writer has put it "Nowhere else in the world, at any time of which there is record, has a helpless, backward people of another color been so swiftly uplifted and so greatly benefited by a dominant race."

The North has no conception of the accomplishment, for it is only where the race is present in large numbers (in the South it makes up over a third of the population) that the problem and the burden really exist. The worst conditions of slavery in the South never approached the horrors from which the American Negro was delivered when he was removed from the slavery of his own race in Africa to slavery under the white man. Wholesale crucifixions to appease the Negro's gods was one of them.

What happens to the Negro even after he has had the advantage of long contact with white men and is then thrown on his own resources is well illustrated by Liberia. Until the League of Nations stopped it, the upper classes there, who had come from America to implant American ideals, enslaved the lower classes. A glance at Haiti is also instructive. Although bolstered constantly by help from the United States, Haitian civilization is little above that of Africa. Illiteracy and poverty among the masses are almost universal. The remains of the earlier French civilization have fallen into ruin. Except where restored by American business enterprise, the bridges and roads are nearly impassable. The religion is Voodoo. Such is the best example available on earth of what a black civilization, led by mulattoes, can acomplish when left to itself.

In the southern United States by way of contrast the Negro lives in greater luxury than many whites in foreign countries. He often drives expensive, white-built motor cars and occupies well-constructed, white-financed houses. In fact, in South Carolina alone more Negroes own automobiles than all the people of Russia, outside of Soviet officials. The Southern Negro has the advantages of white medicine and white-equipped hospitals. If I may cite a further example, we have the case presented by Davis Lee, publisher of a group of Negro newspapers, who writes in the Anderson, South Carolina, Herald:

"Ted Lewis is one of Atlanta's leading Negro businesmen. Some time ago he was having financial difficulty. He went to some of the city's leading Negro businessmen, including the bankers, and tried to borrow $2,500.

"They turned him down flat. He went to the small loan department of the C. & S. Bank. One of the officials went over his plans with him, and then recommended that he borrow $5,000 instead of $2,500. The bank let him have the money without questions. As a result he is a success today, a credit to Georgia and his race."

It is always easy to treat the Negro as an interesting curiosity when there are only a few of him, as is the case in many parts of our North and in many northern European countries. The white man can carry the Negro on his back culturally with little difficulty up to a point. Then he begins to stagger under the load. The South has carried a heavier load better, and farther, than it has ever been carried before. And it has done it through segregation. In fact I know of no case anywhere in the world in which whites have lived with large numbers of blacks without segregation and avoided genocide.

The objectives of the present Negro leadership are, of course, in direct opposition to those of the greatest Negro leader of all time, Booker T. Washington. Although Washington was himself half white, he saw the Negro problem clearly. His position can be stated in his own words: "In all things purely social we can be separate as the fingers, yet one as the hand in all things essential to mutual progress."

A Negro member of the NAACP has written me that the Negro owes nothing to the white man except his troubles. Do you dispute this?

If the Negro likes what our white civilization has to offer, then he should remember that he owes *that* to the white man. Let your correspondent compare his own life in the United States with the life of his African cousins on the Guinea Coast, or in Liberia or Haiti. I should think that if he really feels the way he says he does, he would have enough self-respect to move back to the Guinea Coast, or to Liberia or Haiti, where he can enjoy the native culture of his own race instead of remaining in America and biting the hand that feeds him.

Is not the best way to elevate the Negro to give him a chance to associate socially with white people?

Although such a procedure is basic to the equalitarian philosophy, the best way to lift the inferior up does not lie in pulling the superior down. The white race has had a hard enough time achieving and maintaining its own culture without carrying the sort of burden involved here.[14]

But there is another, more important point. In forcing integration upon the schools of the South, the equalitarians have chosen the most defenseless elements of the community—the children and their under-

14. Consider also the experience of Mr. Robert as cited by Albert Schweitzer in my answer on page 76: "With his abandonment of the social interval between white and black he lost all his influence."

paid teachers—to carry a burden even the strongest should not attempt to bear.

Under the circumstances it is not hard to understand the anger of Southerners, and why it sometimes becomes passion. One of the most unbelievable statements I have read in the American press can be found in the Washington *Post* for June 12, 1959. In commenting upon the withholding of a report on illegitimacy in the District of Columbia, sponsored by the Commissioners Youth Council, the author of the report, one Stanley Bigman, says: "Illegitimacy among Negroes is often a hangover from the life and customs of the slave plantation. Segregation has kept these customs alive . . . there is not much hope of reducing illegitimacy until segregation ends." I would invite Mr. Bigman to examine the Negro's standards of morality in Africa before he was brought to America as a slave, and in Africa or Haiti today where he is on his own, and I would ask Mr. Bigman by what process of reasoning he chooses young white children to be the preceptors of a race but yesterday removed from savagery.

One cannot help wondering how much longer such perversions of all reason and common sense, all principle and morality, as those of Mr. Bigman, are going to be tolerated by the American people.

Are not most Southerners prejudiced?

They are far less prejudiced than Northerners, if we use the word in its true meaning. Prejudice is simply the product of prejudging—that is, of judging before getting the evidence. The South has far more evidence, far more experience, concerning the Negro than the North. And hence it is the North that is pre-judging when it tells the South what it ought to do about the Negro problem.

It makes my blood boil every time I see a Southerner bully, humiliate or exploit a Negro. How can anyone take sides with such people?

Two wrongs don't make a right. The fact that it is wrong to bully, humiliate or exploit a Negro, does not make it right to integrate him. If the North and the court were to spend their time fighting bullies and exploiters, they would accomplish more than by forcing integration.

I will repeat here what I said in my answer to the first question.

My own blood boils at seeing discourtesy to any racial minority. I despise the man who wilfully and without provocation hurts the feelings of others. However, I have witnessed more of this sort of thing toward the Negro in the North than in the South. The South has no monopoly on bullies or unkindness.

I am a Northerner and I sit on hospital and other community boards with Negro doctors and other estimable Negroes. Such people do not seem inferior to me.

Let me point out that not only are these Negroes in no sense typical of their race, whose genes they nevertheless carry and will pass on to their children, but that most of them owe their ability to some percentage of white genes in their system.

It is another characteristic equalitarian deception to introduce the mixed-blood as the true Negro. Plays, moving pictures and TV shows preaching racial equality are built around actors like Harry Bellafonte who had two white grandparents and is consequently half white himself. The equalitarian press is constantly putting forward Ralph Bunche whose deal in genes has been such that he looks like a white man with a light tan. William Faulkner speaks in magazine articles of the achievements of Booker T. Washington whose father was white. George Washington Carver is held up as the ideal Negro scientist but his white genes showed in his blue eyes. Seldom is the true Negro type picked to represent the race in equalitarian propaganda. The North is being spoon fed on a concept of the Negro which is sheer fantasy. Color of skin, of course, is no sure criterion of the degree of white blood. A man may be as black as the ace of spades and still be a mixed-blood with pronounced Caucasoid facial features, relatively high intelligence, and other white attributes.[15]

It must indeed be conceded that the problem of the mixed-blood well over on the white side of the spectrum is one of the most serious

---

15. Blood group studies made during World War II reveal that the composite American Negro, if such a person could be put together from an average taken of gene make-up in the country as a whole, would be 28% white. This does not mean, as some people suppose, that 28% of the Negro population are mixed-bloods. It means that if all American Negro blood could be put into a common pool it would contain 28% white, 72% Negro, genes. Tests by specific areas have not been made. Observation, however, indicates a substantially higher white ratio in the North, and a correspondingly lower ratio in the South.

in the country today. These creatures who, through no fault of their own, often carry in their veins the sinful blood of white men, as one Southerner has put it, are the chief agitators for Negro equality, and who can blame them? May God in his mercy help them to find private solutions to their problems, but let us not mold public policy upon a line which would increase their numbers.

I have dealt recently with representatives of the new African states and found them very sharp. How can these men be considered inferior?

A pure-blooded Negro may surpass a white man in a given situation for one of two reasons. He may belong in what the intelligence testers call the "overlap"—that is, he may be one of the few Negroes who exceed the performance of the average white, although there will be many more whites who exceed this average than there are Negroes. Or he may surpass the white man because the specific intelligence required does not involve the higher centers of self-control, judgment and abstraction. Even a complete savage can be canny in dealings of the latter sort.

But in any case, we must remember that we cannot make a self-sustaining democracy out of a few sharp leaders—it is the average of the electorate that matters. At the risk of monotonous repetition, I must emphasize that the self-control and judgment (the capacity to sacrifice an immediate desire for a greater good tomorrow) of the rank and file, including their willingness to contribute to, rather than to drain, the common treasury, are the qualities which produce a stable, free civilization. These were the qualities which built the great Western democracies. There are few signs of them in Africa.

Ralph McGill, the Atlanta editor, says that the Supreme Court has ordered desegregation but not integration; in other words, it has forbidden the whites to hold the blacks in black schools, but has not ordered the blacks to go to white schools. Isn't this an important distinction?

Not as a practical, long-range matter. It is perhaps true that a large number of Southern Negroes, if left to themselves, would tend for a time to continue in their own schools from inertia and force of habit. But the objectives of the present Negro leadership can be judged by its actions in all the large cities of the United States where it is pressing for more and more Negro attendance in white schools, and challenging token integration wherever it has occurred.

The real meaning of the desegregation movement should be transparent, even to Mr. McGill. It is a main sector of the equalitarian front—piecemeal surrender suits these people perfectly for they understand the truth of what I have said earlier, once a principle is gone, the rest is just a mopping-up operation.

How can we justify second class citizens in the United States?

There have always been first, second, third and various other classes of citizens in the United States, white as well as black, and there always will be, here and in every country, including Russia. But this has nothing to do with segregation. Segregation does not make a second class citizen. If the Negro government of a Negro country decides to segregate all whites in white schools, does this make the whites second class citizens? It is what he is that makes the average Negro a second class citizen, not segregation. And as I have said on page 58, when the day comes that the average Negro is no longer a second class citizen, he may prefer segregation.

Do you not believe in the dignity of man?

I believe in the potential dignity of man, and in its actual existence as the individual acquires it through merit. It is in no way related to segregation. Would white men who had dignity lose it through segregation in a Negro country?

Is not our Society founded on the idea of equal human rights?

All rights have to be limited by the rights of others. My right to do as I please must be limited by your right not to be assaulted by me. The greatest of all human rights is the right of a race to protect itself against genocide, and its culture against deterioration.

How can we condemn a man because of the color of his skin?

Skin color has no bearing on the matter. The Negro's limitations are in the realms of character and intelligence, and the fact they are associated with a black skin is irrelevant. Many Indians of India are blacker by far than many Negroes, yet their culture differs from that of the Negro, and they shun social contact with the Negro.

Are not pride and self-respect essential to the development of personality, and does not segregation deprive the Negro of both?

Did it deprive Booker T. Washington or George Washington Carver of either? Where certain handicaps exist, pride and self-respect grow in overcoming them. They also grow in service and achievement to and within one's own race.

They most emphatically do not grow in forcing one's self where one is not wanted. The latter course is the surest road to loss of self-respect.

Is not discrimination an evil in itself?

No word has been more tarnished by the equalitarian than the word discriminate. Its dictionary definition is "to perceive a difference, to mark a difference". Is that man unjustified who marks a difference between right and wrong, between better and worse? It has become the vogue to condemn discrimination without asking what the reasons for the discrimination may be. Discrimination does not develop in a vacuum. There are always reasons back of it. If the reasons be unsound, then the discrimination ought indeed to be condemned. But if the reasons be sound, then discrimination is a most precious right.

The issue here resembles that raised on page 91. Before a man complains about discrimination or prejudice it would be wise if he asked himself why he is the victim of either.

Should not Americans be tolerant?

Tolerance is a virtue or a vice depending on the situation in which it is exercised. Most certainly we should be tolerant of customs, or ways of life, or opinions that differ from our own provided we believe them to be sincerely followed by men of wisdom and good will. But to be tolerant of evil is either laziness or cowardice.

Are not Southerners racial bigots?

First let us define what we mean by bigot. One of my dictionaries defines it as "One obstinately and irrationally, often intolerantly, devoted to his own church, party, belief or opinion." Another says:

"One who is unreasonably and blindly attached to a particular creed, church, or party; one who is intolerant of opinions which differ from his own; a fanatic; one illiberal or hypocritically stubborn in creed."

We have discused tolerance in the last question. This leaves us with irrationality, blindness and hypocrisy to examine, since obstinacy and fanaticism in a good cause can hardly be considered vices. I have already indicated why I believe the Southern position on race more reasonable by far than that of the North. The North is proving itself both irrational and blind. Lastly, it goes without saying there is no hypocrisy more blantant and vicious than that which forces the children of others into schools with large numbers of Negroes while making sure its own children are well ensconced in schools predominantly of its own race.

Is not the segregationist preaching hate instead of love?

I would say the shoe is on the other foot. It is those who are forcing the Negro into an unnatural relationship with the white race that are guilty of hostile aggression.

Any man or woman who approaches this subject in the spirit of love will find ample ways to help the Negro help himself—which is the only possible road to real betterment—in his own schools and in his own individual and community life. For the North to force him on the white South is as blunt an act of hostility—of hate, if you prefer the word—as can be imagined. It has already damaged the Negro, indeed it is damaging the whole country. The spirit of those back of the integration movement is not love.

Why are Southerners being so emotional?

Here again I would say the shoe is on the other foot. Outside the inner Marxist core, there are very few hard-headed realists among the equalitarians. But there are many sentimentalists, and this has led to the perhaps unfairly sarcastic designation "bleeding heart." The amateur integrationist has been taught to throw the accusation of emotionalism in the face of his opponents to conceal the fact that it is he, himself, whose case lacks reason.

Don't you believe in human progress?

Because I do believe in human progress I protest the gullibility of the Northerner and the Southern "moderate" who are beguiled by the word rather than by the substance of progress, who miss the underlying issue in the integration controversy, and let themselves be ensnared by the old equalitarian technique of gradualism.

The equalitarians have softened us to the point already where many of us think that because something is new it is better. We forget that there are two ways to go forward. One is to go forward up. The other is to go forward down. Humanity will not have progressed by turning the United States a hundred years from now into a nation of octoroons or by making the South mulatto. Nor is any moral victory achieved by submitting the white children of the South to slow cultural poisoning. These are results the Russians devoutly desire, because it will mean that we will no longer need to be reckoned with.

Why try to turn the clock back?

In the first place we aren't dealing with a clock. We are dealing with a pendulum which has swung dangerously far to the left.

In the second place, if it were a clock, I would think it essential to turn it back, if it marked a progression toward disaster. Many a man who has had a bad automobile accident wishes he could turn the clock back to the moment before he made his mistake.

The Constitutional Issue

Does not the spirit of the 14th Amendment require integration?

It is hard to say what the "spirit" of the 14th Amendment is. It can be argued that morally the 14th Amendment is not in the Constitution. All but one of the Southern States rejected it when it was presented to them immediately after the Civil War, and it was only ratified by them when, under a law passed by a Congress from which the South had been excluded, they were given no choice save to accept it or submit to military rule. The President vetoed this law, saying that its whole character, scope and object were without precedent and without authority and in palpable conflict with the plainest provisions of the Constitution. The rump Congress overrode the veto.

The chief proponent of the Amendment, and of the law, was

Thaddeus Stevens, a choleric and vindictive man, egged on by a mulatto mistress who was not unnaturally embittered by her own divided nature. I think historians would agree that if Lincoln had lived, there would have been no 14th Amendment.

Assuming, what many are not willing to assume, that the Amendment has become valid through a sort of unwritten Statute of Limitations, the method of its adoption should clearly have some bearing on the "spirit" in which it ought to be interpreted. Lord Bryce, the great English scholar, in another part of the passage which I quote in my letter to the President, refers to the whole program of the North under this Amendment in Reconstruction days as "monstrous", and modern research has done nothing to change the verdict. Lynching is an abominable crime, but it would be well for the North to remember the conditions which spawned the custom. There were no lynchings until the North drove the white South to the wall by such an orgy of Negro barbarism as had best be forgotten.

More specifically, there was never the slightest suggestion on the part of Congress or anybody else that the Amendment was intended to apply to schools. Congress, having direct control of this matter in the District of Columbia, maintained segregated schools there from the beginning, which is sufficient indication of the intent of the body which proposed the Amendment.

Do not Southerners oppose equality for the Negro largely because they fear their own ascendancy will be challenged?

Yes, and justly so. If your grandparents, as eyewitnesses, had told you of conditions in the South during Reconstruction—of what happens to large aggregations of Negroes under such conditions—or if you had lived awhile in native Negro cultures in Haiti or Africa, you would be afraid, too.

It goes without saying that some progress has been made in the development of the Negro race since the Civil War, but to suppose that it has reached the point where an infusion of color in government amounting to policy control, or to a balance of power, is an acceptable or healthy thing for a previously white society, will be absurd on its face to anyone who has read the answers to the preceding questions. The inclination of Negroes in the mass to be primarily interested in spending rather than conserving their own or other people's money, is but one of many aspects to this problem.

Lord Bryce not only called Northern policy under the Reconstruction Acts monstrous, he noted that no country in the world has ever made such sacrifices of common sense to abstract principle. The South, nevertheless, has managed a workable adjustment within our constitutional frame-work, an adjustment heretofore acceptable to courts wise enough to see the true problem.

I assume you will agree that Lincoln was one of the great exponents of our national democratic principles. Please read the quotation from Lincoln in my letter to the President.

The Dean of the Harvard Law School has said that the trend of previous decisions made the integration decision inevitable. Do you dispute this?

A trend which made the integration decision inevitable was a trend in the wrong direction. But I question whether any trend makes any wrong decision inevitable. If the trend be wrong, it should be stopped. If it be right up to a point, it should be stopped at that point.

I may add in passing that it would be an understatement to remark that the Harvard faculty is not distinguished by the number of conservatives among its members. In fact, the FBI only recently arrested one of them, a man named Zborowski, on a charge of perjury growing out of the Bureau's investigation of a Soviet spy ring. Significantly enough, he had been a research associate in social anthropology.

I may also add that Dr. Harry Emerson Fosdick has fallen a victim to the same illusion as the Dean. He has recently said that "by 1954 the court had dealt with many kinds of separate facilities and found each of them denied equality . . . The court had no choice, in view of the then numerous precedents, but to find that 'separate educational facilities are inherently unequal'."

Both the Dean and Dr. Fosdick have failed to probe down to the underlying issue. *Desegregation in a non-social situation is one thing. Integration in a social situation is quite another.* A trend in one might be justified while in the other it should never be allowed to start. The line, of course, is sometimes hard to draw and is a matter which, under our federal form of government, should be left to local decision. Busses, theaters and restaurants in some communities may readily be distinguished from recreation facilities and schools as regards their social implications; in other communities the distinction may not be as clear.

Is not the decision of the Supreme Court the law, and is it not the duty of every citizen to obey the law?

Unlike the Constitution which is the law of the land, a decision of the Supreme Court is "the law of the case," reversible at will by the members who handed it down, or by other members of the same court at any future date.

My position is that the law in this case ought to be changed, which is a position every citizen is entitled to take.

Some people have asked me how I dare challenge the views of our highest court, and how I can fail to see that loyalty to American ideals requires me to support integration. In all humility I must point to the status of the present court in the opinion of the rest of the judiciary and of the bar. Most certainly the members of this court are honorable men, doing their best, but they cannot be compared with many courts of the past, either in judicial experience or detachment from political considerations.

I question whether any Supreme Court in our history has been the object of a similar indictment at the hands of three-quarters of the State Chief Justices or has stood where this one does in the opinion of the most distinguished members of the bar. If American ideals did not require integration under courts with a superior membership, I fail to see why they require it under the present court.

Isn't opposition really hopeless and isn't it wiser simply to accept integration and make the best of it?

Quite the contrary. The NAACP and the equalitarian press are trying hard to convince the public that the fight is over, but it has just begun. A few figures on where the integration movement stands at the moment may be of interest. The latest statistics I have show that:

In the state of North Carolina, which is being cited throughout the country for taking a creditably moderate course, 39 Negro pupils are enrolled in white schools in seven communities. These 39 are swallowed up among 12,234 white pupils.

Of the 10 other Southern states besides North Carolina, five have some degree of integration and five have none. Among the partially integrated states, Texas has the greatest number of Negro children in white schools—a total of 3,600 colored among 300,000 white in "integrated situations," or about one in a hundred.

Of 1,600 school districts in Texas, only 125—fewer than one in a hundred—have desegrated. It is my understanding that desegregation is mainly in the western part of Texas, which is not typically Southern.

In the other four partially integrated states, here is the score:

Virginia—5 communities, 86 Negroes, 20,327 whites.

Arkansas——8 communities, 94 Negroes, 8,133 whites.

Tennessee—4 communities, 50 Negroes, white total unknown.

Florida—1 community (2 schools), 435 Negroes, 746 whites.

In one of the two Florida schools, token integration has worked in reverse. Five white children are attending Orchard Villa school with 414 Negroes.

For the purpose of comparison then, by omitting Texas and Orchard Villa School in Florida, which are not typical Southern situations, we find that in ten Southern states fewer than 300 Negro children have been admitted to white schools at the present time.

Five states—South Carolina, Georgia, Alabama, Mississippi, and Louisiana—have yet to mix the first school.

Summation And Outlook

You seem to be very sure of your position. Do you see no good among the integrationists, nor any evil on your side?

There is a lunatic fringe to every large controversy. I also believe that many Southerners have allowed their exasperation to drive them to a wildness of expression and action which does harm to their cause. Others trim too much for political and economic reasons. Still others fail to realize that the best answer to the humanitarian integrationist is the even more humanitarian segregationist—more of the Albert Schweitzer spirit toward the Negro.

What I say concerning some Southerners applies equally to many

Northern conservatives, and old-fashioned liberals, in the broader fight against equalitarianism. Too many are embittered men, not without cause, yet unwisely. The younger generations cannot be led back to the great principles by embittered teachers.

There has been a failure of leadership. In his *Revolt of the Masses,* Jose Ortega y Gasset speaks of the current "sovereignty of the unqualified" and I would ask, how far has this been due to the abdication of the qualified, how much of our soft surrender to equalitarianism has derived from a lack of confidence in the old ideals on the part of those who ought to assert and exemplify them?

Near the close of his contemplative autobiography, Lord Tweedsmuir, who knew both the English and the American scenes well, puts this paragraph:

"Something has happened. A civilization bemused by an opulent materialism has been met by a rude challenge. The free peoples have been challenged by the serfs. The gutters have exuded a poison which bids fair to infect the world. The beggar on horseback rides more roughshod over the helpless than the cavalier. A combination of multitudes who have lost their nerve and a junta of arrogant demagogues has shattered the comity of nations. The European tradition has been confronted with an Asiatic revolt, with its historic accompaniment of janissaries and assassins. There is in it all, too, an ugly pathological savour, as if a mature society were being assailed by diseased and vicious children."

These lines, written at the onset of the last World War, would seem to hold fully as true today. The free peoples are still challenged, but the challenge for the moment is more from within than without, the diseased and vicious children have insinuated themselves into our midst and have taken on the trappings of respectability. Some even sit on our university faculties.

As a part of the process, the attack on Christianity, which Gladstone perceived ninety years ago, has continued. "I am convinced," wrote Gladstone, "that the welfare of mankind does not now depend on the State and the world of politics; the real battle is being fought in the world of thought, where a deadly attack is made with great tenacity of purpose and over a wide field upon the greatest treasure of mankind, the belief in God and the Gospel of Christ."

This attack has had a two-fold Asiatic aspect. On the one hand, there has been the open aggression of Japan, Russia, China, and the Middle East, and on the other the indirect impact behind our lines of devious Oriental thinking and the pervasive mood of appeasement, of resignation under evil, and of expediency, so characteristic of the Eastern mind. The it's-too-late attitude—the if-we-must-choose-between-surrender-and-extinction-we'll-choose-surrender spirit—were not the attitude or spirit of our American forefathers, they were not the creed of Patrick Henry.

Part of all this, as I have said, is undoubtedly the fault of an abuse by its votaries of the earlier American gospel. The abuse opened the way, first for a discrediting of freedom and individualism, and then for the substitution of equalitarianism as a new gospel. We cannot afford to make that mistake again. Christianity is the religion of freedom and individualism—it is also the gospel of compassion.

Part, also, of the deterioration, although how much I cannot say, has been due to the appalling loss of the best manhood of the West in two blood-baths in one generation. It is hard to find leadership, hard to find superiority, where the best have been slaughtered by the millions in so short a span. Nevertheless, the deficiency must somehow be made up. The new generations must be brought back to the great principles, the leaders must be found.

The principles, at least, are still before us. I believe most Americans, however short they may fall of the ideal, still hold to the old-fashioned notion that, for every individual, life should be a pilgrimage of self-improvement in mind and character, that today should find a man superior to yesterday and inferior to tomorrow, hence that superiority and inferiority are of the very essence of life and of truth. Every man should scorn equality in the pilgrim stages of himself, and he should scorn it as a social objective. I fail to find any other notion that holds out hope for the progress of either the individual or of society. Equalitarianism spells stagnation and mediocrity for both. I repeat, it is of the very essence of this ideology to build the inferior up by pulling the superior down, and the result is invariably the same. The inferior, in gaining what has not been earned, has lost the spur, and the superior, in losing what was well deserved, has lost the crown.

Isn't the United States supposed to be the great racial melting pot, calling the oppressed of all countries to its shores, and isn't the Statue of Liberty their assurance of welcome?

It is one thing to offer guests a welcome; quite another to have them take over one's house, lock, stock and barrel. This is especially true when the guests have entirely different ideas about housekeeping. The thought back of the original invitation was that the new races would become "Americanized"—not that America would be made over in the image of the new races.

To begin with, the United States was a Christian country. Its language, its literature, its laws and its moral concepts were English. I do not favor its becoming a non-Christian country with a different language, a different jurisprudence and different moral concepts. I oppose this because to change the foundation on which a house is built is a doubtful way to preserve it.

I oppose it also because our English heritage is unique and too precious to be frittered away. Indeed, I am certain that the native English-speaking stocks in the United States, North as well as South, long suffering and gullible as these have been, are at last becoming restive. They are growing tired of watching their public leaders pander to minority groups, playing the majority against itself, and molding policy to suit the minorities. They are sick of seeing words like "freedom" and "democracy" kidnapped and perverted to please every irresponsible element in the community. They are weary of having the ideals of their forefathers derided by the college professors who teach their children. They are surfeited with churchmen who front for communism.[16] They are increasingly suspicious of one-sided newspapers and one-sided publishing houses either controlled by, or pandering to, minority groups. They have had enough of equalitarian propaganda in theater, television and moving pictures.

The greatest danger may well be that when these stocks fully realize the extent to which they have been put upon and betrayed, their resentment may turn to anger harder to control than the depredations of the Marxists.

---

16. I by no means intend to suggest that all college professors or all churchmen are consciously either equalitarians or communists. I believe many, not all, are equalitarian without realizing the implications of their teaching; very few are conscious communists.

Could you give me a few points to stress in my effort to make Northerners realize the situation we face in the South?

I have found it useful to ask nine simple questions. Here they are:

1. Can you name one case in all history in which whites and Negroes in large numbers have lived together without segregation and have failed to intermarry?

2. Can you name one case in all history in which a white civilization failed to deteriorate after intermarrying with Negroes?

3. Can you name one case in all history of a stable, free civilization that was predominantly, or even substantially, Negro?

4. Can you name a better example, anywhere on earth, of a Negro society left on its own resources—after previous local contact with one white civilization and while still under the protection and influence of another such civilization—than the Republic of Haiti, and do you find anything in the Voodoo religion, or the government of Haiti, or its laws, or its public education, or its finances, or its literature, that suggests equality with our white culture?

5. You say the Negro "hasn't had a chance". Going back to the beginning of history, what chances has the white man had that he didn't make for himself, and what chances has the Negro lacked that he couldn't have made for himself, had he had the capacity?

6. You speak of human rights. What human right is greater than the right of a civilization to defend itself against destruction?

7. Did Abraham Lincoln, or Thomas Jefferson, or John Marshall, or Andrew Jackson, or Daniel Webster, or any other great statesman of our past, or any Supreme Court in our history prior to Earl Warren's, favor forcing social integration on the South or consider that its customs in this respect were a denial of equal opportunity or contrary to any other American ideals?

8. Leaving the integration decision aside and considering only general judicial qualifications and capacity, has any Supreme Court in our history ever stood lower in the opinion of the rest of the bench or of the bar than our present Supreme Court?

9. With reference to international appeasement, which is more in the interests of world progress: that an advanced civilization should remodel itself to suit the wishes of backward peoples, or that the

advanced civilization should maintain those policies which have distinguished it from backward peoples?

The whole matter can really be put in a nutshell: a gullible, trusting nation has been misled by various minority groups[17] with their own self-interest at stake into believing that Negroes have an inborn capacity for Western civilization equal to the white race. This has caused the North and the Supreme Court to feel morally justified in forcing the South to risk what amounts to social integration with the Negro. The facts are that the Negro does not have the aforesaid inborn capacity and that social integration with him invariably produces deterioration in any white civilization that tries it. Thus it is not the South which is committing a moral crime against the Negro in maintaining segregation, but the North which is committing a moral crime against the South in forcing integration.

Let me also put the broader problem in a nutshell if I can: The minority groups in question have sown their seed in soil made fertile by the left-wing overdrift of our times. This overdrift has other manifestations. We see it in declining moral standards, in disrespect for distinction and authority, in juvenile delinquency, in the sordid content of literature and the drama, in the appeal of public leaders for votes instead of principles, in the ascendancy everywhere of quantity over quality, in a rising crime rate, in excessive government partiality to labor unions, in the careless workmanship and lack of discipline of the labor force, in the disappearance of the servant class and the resultant waste of higher energies upon domestic duties, in punitive taxation, in the appeasement of evil and lawlessness among men and nations, and in many other aspects of life.

It is an overdrift which sources in one colossal error of fact. There is no such thing as equality in nature.

As is plainly evident, there is no such thing as equality among men. (I acknowledge many men as superior to me, and I mean *superior,* not simply *different.*) To contradict this obvious fact is to set in motion a hornet's nest of evils and to corrupt humanity as a whole. In the United States both the effect of the overdrift and the influence of minorities have been accentuated by the cultural

---

17. I wish again to emphasize here what I said in the last two paragraphs of the answer ending on page 48.

mixing which has taken place since the 1880's, particularly in the urban Northeast and North, which are centers of cultural dissemination for the rest of the country, and in which the mass media have their roots.

Against these things, because of the relative purity of its stocks and traditions, the South is a bulwark.[18] To save the South from integration is to begin the saving of the United States from all the manifestations of equalitarianism and cultural deterioration I have mentioned.

What is the solution to the Negro problem as it shows itself in spheres other than integration?

It should be left to the sovereign states to solve in accordance with the way the issue is presented in each separate area. The whole point in having state governments is to keep questions which have aspects varying with locality in the hands of the people most concerned. States with only a few Negroes have a completely different problem from those with many.

Of course the equalitarian wishes to concentrate matters in Washington, for he can then use the ignorance of large Northern populations to overwhelm the knowledge and experience of the South. But this is not the procedure our Founding Fathers contemplated.

I would point out to you how, throughout the world, men remote from the problem are telling men living with the problem what to do. Doesn't this strike you as rather an inverted state of affairs? Doesn't it strike you as meaningful that the people who are living with the problem always disagree with the people who are not?

Granted it is usually possible, where large populations are involved, for the remote equalitarian to find someone on the local scene to carry his torch for him under the title of "moderate" and wearing the halo of a humanitarian, while the men who are fighting to preserve the integrity of their civilization are variously described as racists, supremacists, rabble or mobs, and pictured as waging a losing battle against the tide of progress. Rest assured,

---

18. It seems to be a favorite technique of equalitarian cartoonists to depict the hillbilly Southerner as the last run of shad in stupidity and depravity. I suggest to these cartoonists that they take one ride in a New York subway.

however, that all the evidence of history points to retrogression where white and black integrate, and that the "progress" offered in this field by the remote Marxist or the local Quisling is a sham. Be not deceived by the efforts of these people to wrap integration up and sell it in the same package with progress in general. Wherever else social revolution may be identified with progress, it cannot be so identified here.

What is the solution to the integration controversy in particular?

There are several possible solutions. In my opinion the Supreme Court has been badly advised, both by the Attorney General and by counsel for the South. The Boas equalitarian anthropology has never been properly examined, the rotten core of this rosy apple, which is the apple upon which integration feeds, has never been laid bare to the judicial eye. I cannot tell, but I would hope that a new case in which this subject was explored might result in a reversal of *Brown vs. The Board of Education.*

It must be admitted that the court handled this aspect of the case in a somewhat unusual fashion. Is is customary for judges to base their decision upon the record of the proceedings. They may take judicial notice of what is common knowledge, such as the fact that the sun rises in the east, but everything else bearing upon the decision must be part of the record so that all parties may have had a chance to argue concerning it.

In the *Brown* case, however, the use of Myrdal's *Dilemma,* and the Boas anthropology on which it is based, was apparently entirely apart from the record and without notice to the parties. In my letter to the Attorney General I said "I assume there must have been some indication, in argument or elsewhere, that these authorities were to be used." I have since been informed that there was no such indication. It may be, therefore, that instead of saying that the court has been badly advised, I should say that the court has not yet given the parties an opportunity to advise it on this important point.

There is also the possibility of a constitutional amendment, but since this requires a vote of three-fourths of the states, the road is long, difficult and doubtful. It is the road the court should have required the integrationist to travel, because, under the Constitution, it is the *change* from established and well-proved ways that was intended to be made hard. It seems certain that an amendment forcing integration upon the South would not have succeeded. Since the court betrayed us all by choosing the wide, easy gate that leads to destruction, it can best lead us back and let the integrationist try the narrow gate.

Basic to either a reversal of the court's decision or to an amendment is the enlightenment of the American people on the real issue. Strong political leadership could accomplish this. A Presidential challenge to the court would be far from unprecedented, and in my judgment could succeed were it supported by a forceful presentation of the facts, and an informed public opinion. The politician who betrays his country as a whole by pandering to a minority group because it appears to hold the balance of power is of all creatures the most pitiful. Leaders in public life seem to have forgotten that if there is one thing the American people love, even sometimes beyond the merits of an issue, it is courage in a public man, and articulate fighting leadership. In this case, fighting leadership would have the merits on its side.

As a practical matter, I think that education of our public men themselves in the essentials discussed here is long overdue. A leader cannot lead when he does not know what the fight is about. Not only must the people of the North be informed, and the brain-washing of thirty years corrected, but our public men must be reached with the facts and persuaded to study them. Once this is accomplished, I am confident the rest will follow rather rapidly. We are actually dealing in this situation with a sort of mass hypnosis in which the bellwethers are fully as hypnotized as the flock.

Far too many Southerners fail to realize that the grounds on which they are basing their resistance, such as states' rights and the Negro's momentary deficiencies, do not go to the heart of the question, however valid in other respects these grounds may be. For example, a Northerner, or a court, can always confuse the point about the Negro's momentary deficiencies with the argument that these can be corrected in the current or next generation and that we must take prompt measures to ensure that they are. When the Southerner pushes the argument beyond this, and questions the momentary nature of the deficiencies, he is met with Boas, and there the debate ends with the North and the court understandably feeling themselves to be the intellectual victors. One cannot win a battle in what Gladstone called "the world of thought" in such a fashion.

Again in the matter of states' rights, while in total agreement with the South on the constitutional question, I believe it a mistake to give it emphasis above, and often to the exclusion of, the issue of limited racial adaptability. If the North and the court feel that a burning wrong is being committed in the name of the Constitution, they will stretch a long way in their interpretation of that document to correct the wrong. Arguments about states' rights fall on unwilling ears, as do references to history and precedent, since the equalitarian replies that the latest scientific discoveries invalidate history and precedent.

Let me suggest an analogy. You are looking out of your door and you see a man on the street corner who appears to be committing murder. You protest, but he replies that he is within his constitutional rights. How much of an impression does he make on you? But now suppose, instead, he answers that he is not committing murder at all, that he is only defending himself against a homicidal attack, is not this the more convincing reply?

The South must win the battle for the mind of the North on moral, not on legal, grounds. It must convince the North that integration is morally wrong because it is destructive of the white civilization of the South. If it fails to do this, then the moral issue immediately moves to the Northern side, and injustice to the Negro becomes the dominant question.

Some fighters in the cause of the South, like David Lawrence, have taken the position that the 14th Amendment is itself illegal. I would not dispute this. But I would point out that the average citizen, reading the simple words of Sec. 1 of this Amendment, would scarcely now find sufficient fault with them, after so much reliance has been placed upon them in so many other situations for so long, to feel that the Amendment should be declared void. In my opinion, the trouble is not with the Amendment but with the new interpretation the court has placed upon it. I would even go so far as to say that if there had been no 14th Amendment the court would have found some other way of accomplishing its purpose.

I am greatly concerned at this unwillingness of the South, and

Northern friends of the South, to meet the racial issue. I think ignorance of the scientific validity of their case partly explains the unwillingness, although innate kindness is also involved, as I have said in my answer to the first question.

I would, therefore, like to see the start of a campaign for the enlightenment of leaders, both North and South, and I would enlarge the word "leader" to include not only public men in the sense of politicians, judges, and other office holders, but all molders of public opinion in the fields of education, religion, journalism and entertainment. It is a strange thing that with the development of modern means of communication those who influence public opinion most are no longer responsible to the electorate. The day when the statesman dominated the public eye and ear has passed. True, the statesman has access to radio and television, as well as to the columns of the press, but this access is small and transient in comparison with the influence exercised by the owners of chains of newspapers and radio and television stations, or national magazines, moving picture companies, and book publishing houses. Such men are responsible to no electorate and can keep on slanting news and warping the public mind long after the statesman in a similar position would have been retired.

While many of these leaders are members of the very minority groups who are seeking to alter the foundations of our society, and from whom consequently nothing can be expected, many are not. The latter, being without instruction, have simply fallen victim to the constant propaganda of the former. The technique of the big lie, endlessly repeated, is a familiar and dangerous one. But it can be counteracted. These men must be reached and informed. Most of them are sufficiently intelligent so that even one attentive reading of Boas, Herskovits, Myrdal or Kluckhohn should be enough.

In addition to a campaign for the enlightenment of leaders, I would recommend the creation of a Foundation for the informing of public opinion as a whole. If millions can be poured into the Carnegie Foundation, and if this Foundation can publish Myrdal's *Dilemma* with its open threat to the pillars of the American way of life, then perhaps some money can be raised to shore those pillars up, something can be spared in defense of the country our forefathers bequeathed us. The functions of such a Foundation are too obvious to be detailed here. Its general object should be to re-educate the American people in the principles upon which our republic was based and through which it grew to greatness. Neither equality nor integration were among them.

In sum, my personal view is that nothing can be accomplished without changing the climate of public opinion in the North, Mid-West, and West, but that this climate can be quickly changed once the core of the issue is made clear, because even without instruction the opinion polls in these areas show a close balance of instinctive judgment on the side of the truth. Thereafter, reversal or amendment is only a question of time. It took experience to produce the repeal of the Prohibition Amendment. In the case of the integration decision we are getting the experience and need only an understanding of the facts.

I have sometimes been told, by those seeking an easier solution, that some sort of compromise must be found, that amendment or reversal "won't do," to which I can only reply: If a patient with a seriously infected appendix goes to a doctor and is advised by the doctor that an operation is imperative, that there is no easier solution, does the patient answer that an operation "won't do"?

Failing a reversal or an amendment, failing an awakened fighting national leadership, there remains only a battle by the South at the local level, a desperate rear guard action which the South will fight perhaps even in some cases to the permanent abandoment of its public schools. But I call upon the North for its own sake to think again before it drives the South any further toward despair or robs its children of their education. In the words of one Southern Senator:

"The Southern whites are in the minority when it comes to determining the policy of the Federal Government; the Negro problem increases yearly; and there are centuries ahead of us. The South needs help, and for the sake of generations yet unborn the South pleads for that help before it is too late. Alone and unaided, Southerners may maintain a white South for many decades yet, and we shall do so in spite of all outside attacks, even those coming from members of our own race whose battles we are also fighting. But the South can hope for no permanent victory over the Negro problem without the aid of the North, East and West . . . This is a problem which the

Nation created and which only the Nation as a whole can adequately and permanently solve."

If, being a Northerner, I may dare to speak one last word to the South, in the utmost sympathy and understanding, I would say, curb your anger as best you can. I am convinced the majority of Northerners are sincere humanitarians who are being unconsciously victimized by a hoax. Work to enlighten them, but do not play into the hands of your enemies, and theirs, by violence. Lynchings and bombings do not destroy these enemies; they destroy you.

Above all, in the face of great provocation, protect the Negro from himself. Continue and improve your stewardship. Give no grounds for the title supremacist. Deserve, as indeed in the past you so often have, the title leader and minister. In the Christian family the Negro is still your younger brother, the figure of the Galilean still stands in judgment over you both.

CHAPTER IV

CONCLUSION

With these answers, as of the end of 1960, I was prepared to rest my case. Reviewing the letters and the replies, there seemed little left to say. In fact, current events, in both the domestic and foreign field, were daily confirming the principles involved.

Unquestionably a major common denominator of fallacy in the many-sided equalitarian ideology was the suppression of the truth concerning the genetic foundation of life. We saw this truth around us every day, in the color of our children's eyes, in the structure of their bones, in the cast of their countenances, in the qualities of mind and heart that paralleled these elements, yet trance-like we clung to the belief that it did not exist. We had every reason to understand that equalitarian scientists would attempt to suppress it, that the equalitarian virus must strike here, if nowhere else, to bring its victims down. Yet in the vogue of the times, the left-wing drift at home, the growth of socialism in Europe, the success of communism in the East, we dropped our guard, lost our discernment, and succumbed.

The fallacy was serious enough in the private world of the individual. It was doubly serious in the world of race. Here blindness moved to the final follies in Little Rock and Leopoldville. Genetic racial limitations should have been as clear as crystal. All history taught it. All free science confirmed it. Few but a patently self-serving minority of trained investigators contested it. Yet the leading nation of the free world embraced the fallacy, used its influence in foreign affairs in support of it, and corrupted its own people in its name.

Tragic as this was, there was a related tragedy that disturbed me fully as much. I had observed the slow erosion by the equalitarian ideology of the minds of otherwise sensible men and women until, while still conceding the fallacy to be a fallacy, they sought escape for their consciences in compromise and appeasement. The cry of "it's-too-late" re-echoed from these defeatists like a knell. I asked myself how far this might be due to a deterioration of the native spirit which founded the nation, and I could only conclude that the explanation lay rather on the borders of the hypnosis. These people were not fully "under"; they were in a half-stupor on the edge. They were sound at heart but slipping into the sleep. I could only say to such victims, "Remember the words of Jesus: 'You will know the truth and the truth will make you free.' Neither you, nor the Negro, nor the nation, nor the world will find freedom or peace or security in fallacies."

Or upon hearing the alternate cry, "But what can we do?" I could only remind the wringers of hands that the answer to that question comes solely to men who have set their faces toward the truth. There are certain journeys on which one is not given, at the start, to see the end. One asks "Which is the path?" and as one walks, the way is revealed. I could give to these a more recent text than the Bible. I could quote the first President of the United States: "Let us erect a standard to which the wise and honest can repair. The event is in the hands of God."

However, a rightful emphasis upon genetic foundations could never preclude an equally rightful emphasis upon environment, and I wondered as I completed my answers whether I had made my position on this point plain. No tendency in human nature is more unfortunate than the tendency to swing from one extreme to another. With the decline of feudal society and the onset of the industrial revolution, men of good will had found themselves first hopeful, then doubtful, then despairing. One form of bondage seemed only to yield to another. Man's exploitation of man continued in new forms. In Europe the new protest took shape in the extremes of Marxism and communism; in America, ameliorated temporarily by the frontier, in the lesser evils of a society increasingly government oriented. Controls that were initiated to curb license were extended to curb liberty. Equality of opportunity, a most precious and characteristically American ideal, was extended to embrace social, cultural and genetic equality. Error had used the door of pity to enter both our minds and hearts. Environment had been counted upon to accomplish everything, and in the process the general environment had, perforce, declined.

Must I then urge, or seem to urge, a swing toward an exclusively genetic emphasis? Must I be held to condone inferior schools, slums, unnecessary segregation in non-social situations, and humiliating attitudes toward the Negro? Prayerfully not. For every ounce of emphasis on heredity, I favored precisely an ounce of emphasis on environment, provided it were an environment, for white and black alike, which contained inducements to self-reliance rather than to government dependence, and to the earning of status rather than to a presumption of title. Only the raw material was genetic. It determined the limits. What was built within those limits depended on the environment. Good raw material, with nothing built, yielded nothing. Limited raw material with careful building might yield much. There was no denying that the vital force in the soul of a man needed challenge. The distinction that had to be drawn was between the challenge and the millstone.

The environment had indeed declined in its inspirational values, conformity had replaced initiative, security had eclipsed enterprise. It was impossible forever to glorify the underdog without in the end glorifying too much of what the underdog stood for, just as one could not incessantly disparage distinction without in the end destroying excellence. But a vast task remained in creating an inspirational environment for those willing and able to benefit from it. Social justice in such an environment was harder to achieve than social security.

In the case of the Negro it was imperative to remember, in the words of the great French anthropologist Millot, that the limitation was "one of degree and not of nature". The essential humanity in the Negro must never be forgotten. Cooperation, the bonds of loyalty and affection, in their appropriate spheres, were wholly natural and desirable. It was worth recalling the words of Booker T. Washington, " In all things purely social we can be separate as the fingers, yet one as the hand in all things essential to mutual progress". The ideal of racial integrity did not preclude the ideal of a common humanity. Men of good will, both North and South, both black and white, had always known this. Save for the intrusion of alien influences, they would have continued the progress that had already exceeded any made before.

The Negro in his heart was fully aware of his debt. Since he did not wish to return to Africa, he had the duty to remember, as did all those who were enjoying the blessing of American life, that it had flowered from the blood, the intelligence and the character of men long schooled and experienced in the responsibilities of freedom. If the Negro wished to share in its benefits, let him not undertake to destroy their source, nor to be made a tool by white men of alien background and design.

The man with the heaviest burden to carry, the man who could do the most harm and also the most good—the man who must choose between avenging or redeeming a past beyond his control—was the mixed-blood. To him, every white man of good will owed a particular obligation. No class of our citizens were entitled to higher respect than those mulattoes who chose to redeem the past, just as none were to be more shunned than those who chose to avenge it. In the North there were untold numbers who had the alternative. There were many in the South. Wherever they were and in whatever degree their ability and character deserved, let white men open the door of opportunity to them with a special sympathy. Even for them, the white man could not, if he were wise, deny the genetic truth. But he could lighten the burden.

The mulatto who was bent on making the nation mulatto was the real danger. His alliance with the white equalitarian often combined men who had nothing in common save a belief that they had a grudge against society. They regarded every Southerner who sensed the genetic truth as a bigot and used every tactic of deceit and every balance-of-power position to teach and vote a genetic fallacy. Here were the men who needed to be reminded of the debt the Negro owed to white civilization. If Africans were to be brought to America to observe and learn, let such mulattoes be taken to the Congo to observe and learn.

Even here, however, I could not urge a spirit of hostility. Steadfastness against false teachings, but understanding of how such teachings were motivated, was imperative. A little imagination sufficed to recognize the difficulties and temptations, even of the avengers. Firmness was not incompatible with compassion.

As I shuffled the last of these pages on my desk, an October afternoon was ending and, at the country place where I live, the fall air was scented with the smoke of burning leaves. There is always in our American autumn, it seems to me, a quality of appraisal and rededication, and on this afternoon I felt how much we needed an inventory of the values that had made us great. Minority groups, coming to us for asylum out of centuries of failure in the struggle for freedom, clamored to dilute those values, but their voices only made the more necessary our own recommitment. I could only repeat: To alter the foundations on which a house is built is a doubtful way to preserve it. Let us continue building, let us extend the foundations, but let us not change rock to sand.

INDEX

"As a result of recent findings in the fields of physiological genetics and population genetics, particularly as concerns blood groups, the applicability of both the inequality axiom and the exclusion principle is rapidly becoming accepted. . . . The emotional restrictions of rational discussion in this field are immense. . . . It is not sadism or masochism that makes us urge that the denial be brought to an end. Rather, it is a love of the reality principle, and recognition that only those truths that are admitted to the conscious mind are available for use in making sense of the world."

Garrett Hardin in *Science*, April 29, 1960